The Leaseholders Handbook

Key Advice Guides
MARTIN LEVY

Key Advice Guides

Key Advice Guides
38 Cromwell Road
London E17 9JN

ISBN 1900694 02 6

Printed and bound by Bookcraft Limited.

Cover design by Straightforward Graphics

The Leaseholders Handbook

CONTENTS

Introduction

INTRODUCTION

Over the last 30 years, the law covering leasehold property has developed in a manner which has given more and more protection to leaseholders. This protection was seen as necessary because all too often leaseholders have been victims of poor management by (often) unscrupulous landlords, particularly in the area of service charge delivery and management of service charge accounts.

In the public sector, there has been a marked lack of knowledge and resultant management problems, particularly in the area of service charges, and only now has it been seen as necessary to promote this area as a specialism.

Since the 1960' s, laws have been introduced designed to provide a regulatory framework for the dealings between freeholder and leaseholder, initially concerning the acquisition of the freehold of properties, by leaseholders, and in the 1980's in the area of the provision of service charges and overall management. The 1985 Landlord and Tenant Act, as amended by the 1987 Landlord and Tenant Act, provides for a series of steps which landlords must observe when spending service charge money of leaseholders in their blocks

It is surprising how many freeholders and leaseholders live in ignorance of their rights and obligations, even though such a significant body of legislation exists to protect those rights.

In 1993, the Leasehold Reform and Urban Development Act extended those rights initially granted in the 1967 Leasehold Reform Act to the purchase of the freehold and extension of leases. Collectively, leaseholders can purchase the freehold of a block (enfranchisement) and individually leaseholders can extend their leases by a given number of years past its existing life. These steps are clear but can be problematic and are described in full in this book.

In May 2002, the Government introduced the Commonhold and Leasehold Reform Act, which introduces new legislation protecting leaseholders and amends the 1993 Leasehold Reform Act. This Act introduces the ' no fault' right to manage where, subject to certain

4

criteria leaseholders can take over the running of their flats, without having to prove fault. The Act is discussed in detail in chapter five.

The general principles covering the setting up of a flat management company, and how to run a company effectively, are also outlined. This is a natural follow on to the acquisition of the freehold of a block, whether by enfranchisement or voluntary sale.

Overall, the book is designed to raise the awareness of leaseholders who wish to understand what is often a complex relationship between landlord and tenant, and also to help landlords understand their own obligations.

There is a detailed appendix in the book which covers the Landlord and Tenant Act 1985 (as amended) and also gives examples of the necessary paperwork required in the setting up of a management company, such as the memorandum and articles of association. There are also draft model service charge budget and accounts.

1

THE LEASE - WHAT IT IS AND HOW IT WORKS

Freehold and Leasehold

The strongest form of title to land is that of freeholder. Freehold title lasts for ever; it may be bought and sold, or passed on by inheritance.

Freeholders can use their land for other purposes. They may also, if they wish, allow other people to use their land, usually though a lease or tenancy.

A lease grants the leaseholder permission to use the land for a certain period, which can be anything from a day or two to several thousand years. It will usually attach conditions, for example that the leaseholder must pay rent (usually a sum of money). The lease may, but does not have to, put certain restrictions on what the leaseholder may do with the land. But it must, in order to be a lease rather than merely a licence, grant the leaseholder 'exclusive possession'. This is the right to exclude other people, especially the landlord, from the land. Such a right need not be absolute, and exceptions to it are explained later in the book: but it is enough to give the leaseholder a high degree of control over the land, which has become, for the duration of the lease, very much the leaseholder's land rather than the freeholder's. A lease, unless it contains a stipulation to the contrary, may be bought, sold, or inherited; if this happens, all the rights and duties under it pass to the new owner.

Leases and Tenancies

Confusion is often caused by the fact that, although the terms leaseholder (or lessee) and tenant are legally interchangeable, they leaseholder (or lessee) and tenant are legally interchangeable, they tend to be used in different senses. The tendency is to refer to short leases as tenancies: the more substantial the rights conferred, and the longer the period for which they run, the more likely it is that the agreement will be referred to as a lease.

It is common for private landlords to insist on prepayment of rent or a deposit before granting a tenancy, and almost all landlords will levy a service charge to cover the cost of some activities that a peripheral to the central one of providing housing; but despite these costs it would be true to say that the principal financial responsibility accepted by a periodic or short-term tenant is that of paying the rent.

The position of a leaseholder is very different. The major financial commitment will usually be a substantial initial payment either to the landlord (if the lease is newly created) or to the previous leaseholder. This is normally done through a mortgage. There is still a rent, called a ground rent, payable to the landlord, but it is usually a notional amount (£50 a year is not uncommon). Its purpose is not so much to give the landlord an income as to give the leaseholder an annual reminder that ultimate ownership of the land is not his.

Different types of Leasehold Property
The great majority of leases relate to flats rather than houses. Where flats are sold, each purchaser acquires a lease that gives him specified rights over the parcel of land on which the flats stand. These rights, of course, are shared by the leaseholders of the other flats. In addition, however, each leaseholder gains the right to exclusive possession of part of the building occupying the land - his own flat.

The freehold of flatted property will often be retained by the developer, although sometimes it will be sold to a property company. Formerly, it was common practice for the freehold to be retained even when separate houses were built. This allowed the freeholder to retain an interest in the property and, above all, to regain full possession of it when the lease expired. However, the position of freeholders has been weakened by two key pieces of legislation, the Leasehold Reform Act 1967 and the Leasehold Reform, Housing and Urban Development Act 1993, both of which have now been extended by the Housing Act 1996. These Acts are described in detail in Chapter Four: their overall effect is to entitle leaseholders either to the freehold of houses or to a new lease of flats. In view of the legislation, there is now little point in the original owner attempting to retain the freehold of land on which houses have been built. The exception is where a house is sold on the basis of shared ownership - see below.

Most residential leasehold property therefore consists of flats. Of these, most are in the private sector, comprising purpose-built blocks and (especially in London) conversions of what were once large single houses. The freehold will usually belong to the developer, to a property company, or sometimes to the original owner of the site.

House leases normally give most of the repairing responsibility to the leaseholder - services provided by the freeholder, and therefore service charges, are minimal. In flats, however, although the leaseholder will normally be responsible for the interior of the flat, the freeholder will maintain the fabric of the building and will recoup the costs of doing so by levying service charges on the leaseholders. This is an area of such potential conflict between leaseholders and freeholders that it has been the subject of legislation, which is discussed further on in the book.

The right to buy

The general shift from renting to owning means that sometimes flats have been sold in blocks that were originally developed for letting to tenants: the result is often a 'mixed-tenure' block, with both leaseholders and tenants. Although this sometimes happens in the private sector, it is particularly common in blocks owned by local authorities and housing associations, for it is to these that the statutory right to buy applies. This right was created by the Housing Act 1980 and allows local authority tenants, and some housing association tenants, to buy their homes at a heavily discounted price. Tenants of houses are normally sold the freehold, but tenants of flats become leaseholders.

More recently, a similar but less generous scheme has been introduced covering many housing association tenants not already qualifying for the full right to buy.

Purchasing a council home has been, for most of the million or so that have done so, a very satisfactory investment. A minority of purchasers have, however, met with serious difficulties, particularly where they have become leaseholders in mixed tenure blocks of flats: Chapter Three looks at some of the problems affecting management and service charges.

Shared ownership

Another result of the trend towards home ownership has been the dramatic expansion of shared ownership. This is a form of tenure that combines leasing and renting. However, the term 'shared ownership' is something of a misnomer because ownership is not, in fact, shared between the leaseholder and the freeholder. The lease relates to the whole property, not part of it, and the shared owner is as entitled as any other leaseholder to consider himself the owner of his house. The key point about shared ownership leases is not that they give an inferior form of tenure to other leases but that they have different conditions attached. The leaseholder pays less than the full value of the lease; typically, half. In exchange for this concession, he pays not the normal notional ground rent but a much more substantial rent. However, he is much more a leaseholder than he is a tenant, and, like other leaseholders (but unlike tenants) is responsible for the internal repair of the property and, in the case of houses, usually the fabric of the building too.

Shared owners usually have the right to increase their stake as and when they can afford it: this is called 'staircasing' because the owner's share goes up in steps. If the property is a house, the freehold will normally be transferred when the owner's share reaches 100%, and he will then be in the same position as any other freehold home owner. If it is a flat, he will continue to be a leaseholder but there will no longer be a rental (other than ground rent).

Head Leases and Subleases

It is the right of the leaseholder, unless the lease specifically forbids it, to sublet the property, or part of it, to someone else. This means that the leaseholder has delegated some of his rights over the property to another person. Obviously, he cannot delegate rights greater than his own, and he cannot grant a sublease of the whole of his rights because this would leave him with no interest in the property: it would, in fact, amount to the same as an assignment (see Chapter Two). So it is necessary for a sublease that the original leaseholder be left with something; either some period of time or some part of the property.

2

RESPECTIVE OBLIGATIONS OF FREEHOLDER AND LEASEHOLDER

For centuries the law did little to regulate the relationship between freeholders and leaseholders. The view was taken that they had entered into the relationship of their own free will, and it was up to them to agree whatever terms and conditions they liked.

In the twentieth century, however, the view has grown up that some types of bargain are inherently unfair and even those that are not may still be open to exploitation.

An example of the first type is an agreement that residential property will revert to the original freeholder at the end of a long lease. This meant that when 99-year leases expired, leaseholders found that their homes had abruptly returned to the outright ownership of the heir of the original freeholder, leaving them as mere trespassers liable to be ejected at any time. In practice, freeholders were usually willing to grant a fresh lease, but sometimes only at a very high price that the leaseholder might well be unable to afford. In some cases, freeholders insisted on reclaiming the property however much the leaseholder offered, and the law supported them. This is the state of affairs that led to legislation entitling almost all residential leaseholders to extend their leases, and many of them to claim the freehold. This is dealt with in Chapter Four.

The freeholder's right to demand a service charge is an example of an arrangement that is fair in principle but open to abuse in practice. It is inevitable, especially in flats, that responsibility for some types of repair cannot be ascribed to any individual leaseholder and must therefore be retained by the freeholder; who must, in turn, recoup the cost from leaseholders. However, some freeholders abused this system by levying extravagant service charges that made the service system by levying extravagant service charges that made the service charge as a source of profit. To prevent this, there is now a substantial body of legislation designed to ensure that freeholders carry out only the works that are really necessary and that they recover their legitimate costs and no more. The complicated rules governing this are chiefly found in the *Landlord and Tenant Act 1985 (as amended) and the Housing Act 1996 and are described in Chapter Three.*

Under the Landlord and Tenant Act 1987, AS AMENDED BY THE Commonhold And Leasehold Reform Act 2002, either party to a long lease (one originally granted for at lease 21 years) may go to court (or Leasehold Valuation Tribunal under the new Act) to argue that the lease is deficient in some way and needs to be changed. If only the one lease is affected, the court may vary it. Sometimes, however, a number of leases may need to be changed; in this case either the freeholder or 75% of the leaseholders may apply.

Where the law is silent, however, it remains the case that the lease can contain any covenants or conditions that the freeholder can induce the leaseholder to accept.

Obligations of Leaseholders

Leases have been drawn up at different times and vary depending on prevailing legal practice and on the chief concerns of the freeholder at the time. However, similar terms are found in typical leases

a: Onerous conditions

This is a term applied to conditions that have the effect of seriously reducing the value of the lease. Such a condition is not necessarily an unreasonable one; it may serve some legitimate purpose. But no one should sign a lease containing them without fully understanding their likely effect.

A common example of an onerous term is a restriction on the

kind of person to whom the lease may be sold (or 'assigned' - see below). For example, a housing scheme may have been intended specifically for the elderly. Clearly, it could not be maintained as such if leaseholders were free to assign or bequeath their leases to whomever they please, so the lease will say that it may be assigned only to persons above a certain age, and that if it is inherited by anyone outside the age group it must be sold on to someone qualified to hold it. Although this could be described as an onerous term because it makes it more difficult to find a buyer and may reduce the lease's value, it is reasonable given the need to ensure that the scheme continues to house elderly people exclusively. And the restriction it imposes is not too severe because so many potential purchasers qualify.

However, some leases define much more narrowly to whom they may be sold. Sometimes the freeholder is a body owned and run by the leaseholders themselves, and in these cases it is usual to require that all leaseholders must join the organisation and, if they leave it, must immediately dispose of the lease to someone that is willing to join. Again, such a term is not necessarily unacceptable. If the organisation makes relatively light demands on its members (perhaps no more than a modest admission fee or annual subscription), the restriction is unlikely greatly to diminish the value of the lease. If, however, the organisation expects much more from its members - perhaps that they actively take part in running it, or that they pay a large annual subscription - the value of the lease will be severely reduced because it will be difficult to find purchasers willing to accept the conditions. A key point is whether the organisation has power to expel members, thus forcing them to sell; and, if so, in what circumstances and by whom this power can be exercised.

b: Blanket conditions

Slightly different from the onerous condition is the blanket condition. It is common for leases to contain sweeping provisions that would, if they were enforced, give the freeholder considerable control over the leaseholder's life. For example:

- *Pets* Leases often lay down that the leaseholder may not own pets, or may not do so without the freeholder's permission.

- *Business Leases* often lay down that the leaseholder must not run any sort of business from his home.

- *Use as residence.* A lease will generally say that the property is to be used for residential purposes, and will sometimes attempt to restrict how many people may live there apart from the leaseholder.

It is easy to see why freeholders want such clauses in the lease. But the kind of blanket rules that appear in many leases go too far. A rule against any pets at all forbids not only noisy dogs but also inoffensive pets such as a budgie or a goldfish. In the same way, prohibiting business activities means that the leaseholder may not use his home to write a book for publication, or address envelopes, and so on - types of homeworking that could not possibly inconvenience anyone.

The reality is that this kind of provision is seldom enforced. Freeholders, and their lawyers, like it because they feel that it preserves their freedom of action, allowing them to decide whether or not to enforce the lease if it is clear that one of these blanket conditions is being broken..

c: Access

Virtually any lease will contain a clause allowing the freeholder to enter the property in order to inspect or repair it. This has the effect of qualifying the leaseholder's right of exclusive possession (see Chapter One), but only subject to certain conditions. The freeholder (or the freeholder's servants, such as agents or contractors) may enter only at reasonable times, and subject to the giving of reasonable notice. If these conditions are not met, the leaseholder is under no obligation to allow them in; and, even when the conditions are met, the landlord will be trespassing if he enters the property without the leaseholder's consent.

If the leaseholder refuses consent even though the time is reasonable and reasonable notice has been given, the landlord's remedy is to get a court order against the leaseholder compelling him to grant entry. It is probable, in such a case, that the landlord will seek, and get, an award of legal costs against the leaseholder.

Obligations of Freeholders
Exclusive possession and quiet enjoyment
The first and most important obligation on the freeholder, without which there would be no legal lease at all, is to respect the leaseholder's rights of 'exclusive possession' and 'quiet enjoyment'. Exclusive possession is as the right to occupy the property and exclude others from it, especially the freeholder. Quiet enjoyment is another way of underlining the leaseholder's rights over the property: it means that the freeholder may not interfere with the leaseholder's use of the property provided that the terms of the lease are observed.

However, the leaseholder's right to quiet enjoyment applies only to breaches by the freeholder or the freeholder's servants such as agents or contractors. It is important to note this because the term is sometimes thought to mean that the freeholder must protect the leaseholder against any activity by anyone that interferes with his use of the property: this is not so. For example, if the freeholder carries out some activity elsewhere in the building that interferes with the leaseholder, the leaseholder's right to quiet enjoyment has been breached and he is entitled to redress unless the freeholder can show that the activity was necessary, for instance to comply with repairing

17

obligations under the lease. But if the interference is caused by someone else, perhaps another leaseholder, the freeholder's obligation to provide quiet enjoyment has not been breached. And it is worth stressing in this connection that even if the other leaseholder is in breach of his lease, it is entirely up to the freeholder whether or not to take action: other leaseholders have no power to force the freeholder to deal with the situation.

The 'section 48' notice

Another important protection for leaseholders is found in section 48 of the Landlord and Tenant Act 1987. This was designed to deal with the situation in which freeholders seek to avoid their responsibilities by (to put it bluntly) doing a disappearing act. Sometimes freeholders would provide no address or telephone number or other means of contact, meaning that leaseholders were unable to hold the freeholder to his side of the agreement. Sections 47 and 48 therefore lay down that the freeholder must formally notify the leaseholder of his name and give an address within England and Wales at which he can be contacted, and that this information must be repeated on every demand for rent or service charge. This has proved especially valuable for leaseholders where the freeholder lives abroad, or is a company based abroad. It should be noted that the address does not have to be the freeholder's home, nor, if the freeholder is a company, its registered office; often it will be the address of a solicitor or property management company, or simply an accommodation address. But the key point is that any notice, or legal writ, is validly served if sent to that address, and the freeholder is not allowed to claim that it never came to his notice.

Good management

The freeholder is under an obligation to ensure that his management responsibilities are carried out in a proper and appropriate way. Leaseholders can take the freeholder to court if they believe they can show that they are not receiving the standard of management to which they are entitled. This may be an expensive and lengthy process but it better than the alternative, sometimes resorted to by leaseholders, of withholding rent or service charge. This is risky because, whatever the shortcomings of the freeholder's management, it puts the leaseholders in breach of the conditions of their lease and, as such, demonstrably in the wrong (even if the freeholder may be in the wrong as well).

It may be that leaseholders need more information so that they can decide whether the management is satisfactory. If so, there is power under the Leasehold Reform, Housing and Urban Development Act 1993 for a management audit to be demanded by an auditor acting on behalf of at least two-thirds of the qualifying leaseholders. Qualifying leaseholders are those with leases of residential property originally granted for 21 years or more and requiring them to contribute to the cost of services. The purpose of the audit, the costs of which must be met by the leaseholders demanding it, is to discover whether the freeholder's duties are being carried out efficiently and effectively. The auditor is appointed by the leaseholders and must be either a qualified accountant or a qualified surveyor and must not live in the block concerned. The auditor has the right to demand papers from the freeholder and can go to court if they are not produced.

In extreme cases a leaseholder can use the Landlord and Tenant Act 1987 to force the appointment of a managing agent to run the block instead of the freeholder. The leaseholder must serve a notice telling the freeholder what the problems are and warning that unless they are put right a Leasehold Valuation Tribunal will be asked to appoint a managing agent. The LVT may make such an order if it satisfied that it is 'just and convenient'; the Act mentions, as specific examples where this may apply, cases where the freeholder is in breach of obligations under the lease and cases where service charges are being levied in respect of work of a poor standard or an unnecessarily high standard. It should be noted that this procedure, although in some ways it resembles the procedures for collective enfranchisement in Chapter Five, differs from them in that it can be carried out by any individual leaseholder; it does not require the consent of a majority. Note too that the procedure is not available if the freeholder is a local authority, a registered housing association, or the Crown.

A recognised tenants' association (RTA), where there is one, has additional rights to be consulted about managing agents. The RTA can serve a notice requiring the freeholder to supply details of the managing agent and the terms of the management agreement. Recognised tenants' associations are more important, however, in connexion with service charges, explained in the Chapter Three.

Leaseholders that are receiving a consistently poor or overpriced service may also wish to consider getting rid of the freeholder altogether by collective enfranchisement under the Leasehold Reform, Housing and Urban Development Act 1993 (see Chapter Four). In addition, there is now the right to manage without proving fault, which is contained in the Commonhold and leasehold Reform Act 2002. We will be discussing this Act in more depth in chapter 5.

Assignment of Leases

One of the most important characteristics of a lease - in marked contrast to most tenancies - is that it may be bought and sold. Usually, the freeholder has no say in this: the leaseholder may sell to whom he likes for the best price he can get, provided that the purchaser agrees to be bound by the terms of the lease. It is, however, usual for the lease to lay down that the freeholder must be informed of any change of leaseholder.

What actually happens when a lease is sold is that the vendor agrees to transfer to the buyer his rights and obligations under the lease. This is called 'assignment' of the lease. In some types of housing the freeholder has the right to intervene if an assignment is envisaged. The housing may, for instance, be reserved for a particular category of resident, such as the retired, so the freeholder is allowed to refuse consent to the assignment if the purchaser does not qualify.

It was mentioned above that the assignee takes over all the rights and responsibilities attaching to the lease. This means, for instance, that he takes responsibility for any arrears of service charge. This is why purchasers' solicitors go to such lengths to ensure that no arrears or other unusual obligations are outstanding.

If the Lease Is Breached

If the terms of a lease are broken, the party offended against can go to court. This may be the leaseholder, for instance if the freeholder has failed to carry out a repair. But it is normally the freeholder that takes the leaseholder to court, for failure to pay ground rent or service charges or for breach of some other requirement.

It is for the court, if satisfied that the lease has been breached, to decide what to do. The normal remedy will be that the offending party must pay compensation and that the breach (if it is still continuing) must be put right. It is also likely that the loser will be obliged to pay the winner's legal costs as well as his own, a penalty often considerably more severe than the requirement to pay compensation.

A much more severe remedy open to the freeholder if the leaseholder is in breach is forfeiture of the lease. This means what it says: the lease is forfeited to the freeholder. Forfeiture is sometimes threatened by the more aggressive class of freeholder but the good news for leaseholders is that in practice courts have shown themselves loathe to grant it except in very serious cases.

Since the Housing Act 1996 took effect, and recently the 2002 Commonhold and Leasehold Reform Act, forfeiture for unpaid service charges has been made more difficult for freeholders; this is covered in the next Chapter.

Where forfeiture is threatened for any reason other than failure to pay rent (which means the basic rent, not the service charge element), the freeholder must first serve a 'section 146 notice', so called after the relevant provision of the Law of Property Act 1925. In this he must state the nature of the breach of the lease, what action is required to put it right; if he wants monetary compensation for the breach, the notice must state this too. If the notice is not complied with, the freeholder may proceed to forfeit; but the leaseholder may go to court for relief from forfeiture.

The breach of the lease specified in the section 146 notice must have occurred during the twelve years preceding the notice. For breaches older than this, no valid section 146 notice can be served and so forfeiture is not available.

If the freeholder breaches the lease, the leaseholder can go to court and seek an order requiring the freeholder to remedy the breach, to pay damages, or to do both. The commonest type of breach complained of by leaseholders is failure to carry out repairs, and this explains why action by leaseholders is less usual; they know that if they force the freeholder to do repairs the costs will be recovered through service charges. Legal action may be the best course if the dispute affects a single leaseholder: but if a number of leaseholders are involved they may well prefer to get rid of the freeholder altogether by collectively enfranchising their leases as described in Chapter Four.

3

SERVICE CHARGES AND THE LAW

By far the commonest cause of dispute between leaseholders and freeholders is the provision of services and the levying of service charges. In extreme cases, leaseholders have been asked to contribute thousands of pounds towards the cost of major repairs, and have even suffered forfeiture of the lease if they are unable, or unwilling, to comply. Happily, such instances are rare; but even where the service charges are more moderate, they are often resented by leaseholders.

The landlord of rented property is expected to meet virtually all costs from the rent, whereas the freeholder of leasehold stock has no rent to fall back on (apart from the normally negligible ground rent). How, then, are major costs to be met when they arise? The answer, of course, is from the service charge, which is, therefore, of central importance to the management of leasehold property.

From the freeholder's point of view, the logic of service charges is impeccable. It is perfectly reasonable for freeholders to point out:

- that leaseholders benefit from the work because it has maintained or improved their homes; and
- that the fact that the work has been done means that leaseholders will get a better price when they come to sell; and
- that people that own their homes freehold have to find the money to meet costs of this kind.

In short, the purchase of a lease means the acceptance of a commitment to pay the appropriate share of costs.

But this does not mean that leaseholders have no scope to

But this does not mean that leaseholders have no scope to challenge or query service charges. Under sections 18 to 30 of the Landlord and Tenant Act 1985, as amended, and also the 1996 Housing Act and, recently, the 2002 Commonhold and Leasehold Reform Act they have extensive legal protection against improper or unreasonable charging by freeholders, and this is discussed later in the Chapter. First, however, we should look at how a typical service charge is made up.

What goes into a Service Charge?

The lease will say how often service charges are levied: typically, six-monthly or annually. It is usual to collect the ground rent at the same time, but this is usually a fairly small component of the bill. The service charge proper will normally consist of three elements.

- **The management fee** is the charge made by the freeholder, or the freeholder's agent, to cover the administrative cost of providing the service and collecting the charge. Usually it will be much the same amount from one year to the next, but if major works have occurred the management fee will usually be higher to cover the extra costs of appointing and supervising contractors; 15% of the cost of the works is a common figure.

- **Direct costs (routine expenditure)** cover costs such as the supply of electricity to communal areas, building insurance, and the like. Again, these costs are likely to be fairly constant from year to year, so leaseholders know in advance roughly how much they are likely to have to pay.

- **Direct costs (exceptional expenditure)** cover costs that are likely to be irregular but heavy. They usually result from maintenance and repair, and it is because this component of the service charge is so unpredictable that it gives rise to so many problems. Where a house has been divided into leasehold flats, the freeholder's costs will usually be similar to what a normal home owner would be obliged to pay; in other words, the costs may well be in the thousands (for a new roof, say) but are unlikely to be higher. Even so, a charge of £5000 for a new roof, even if divided between three or four flats, is still a major cost from the point of view of the individual leaseholder, especially if it is unexpected. The situation can be far worse in blocks of flats, where the costs of essential repair and maintenance may run into millions. Replacement of worn-out lifts, for example, is notoriously costly; and costs arising from structural defects are likely to be higher still.

Unreasonable Service Charges
General Principles
Sections 18 to 30 of the Landlord and Tenant Act 1985, as amended by the Landlord and Tenant Act 1987, grant substantial protection to leaseholders of residential property. (See appendix 1) This protection was introduced after complaints of exploitation by unscrupulous leaseholders, who were alleged to be carrying out unnecessary, or even fictitious, repairs at extravagant prices, whilst not providing the information that would have enabled leaseholders to query the bill. The effect of the Act is to require freeholders to provide leaseholders with full information about service charges and to consult them before expensive works are carried out.

A few leases, namely those granted under the right to buy by local authorities or registered housing associations, have some additional protection under the Housing Act 1985 (see below), but sections 18 to 30 apply to all residential leases where the service charge depends on how much the freeholder spends. They set out the key rules that freeholders must observe in order to recover the cost, including overheads, of 'services, repairs, maintenance or insurance', as well as the freeholder's costs of management.

It should be noted that failure by leaseholders to pay the service charge does not relieve the freeholder of the obligation to provide the services. The freeholder's remedy is to sue the leaseholder for the outstanding charges, or even to seek forfeiture of the lease (see below).

Section 19 of the Act provides the key protection to leaseholders by laying down that service charges are recoverable only if they are 'reasonably incurred' and if the services or works are of a reasonable standard. This means that the charge:

- must relate to some form of 'service, repair, maintenance, or insurance' that the freeholder is required to provide under the lease;
- must be reasonable (that is, the landlord may not recover costs incurred unnecessarily or extravagantly);
- may cover overheads and management costs only if these too are reasonable.

In addition, the charge must normally be passed on to the leaseholders within 18 months of being incurred, and in some cases the freeholder must consult leaseholders before spending the money. These points are covered below.

The Housing Act 1996 (amended by the 2002 Commonhold and Leasehold Reform Act 2002) gave leaseholders new powers to refer service charges to the Leasehold Valuation Tribunal (LVT). This is covered below (*Challenging Service Charges*).

Leasehold Valuation Tribunals operate throughout England and Wales. They are appointed jointly by the Lord Chancellor and (in England) the Environment Secretary and (in Wales) the Welsh Secretary. They perform a large number of quasi-judicial functions in relation to property, especially leasehold property, and will feature frequently in the remainder of the book.

Consultation with Leaseholders

Section 20 of the LTA 1985 provides extra protection where the cost of works is more than £50 per leaseholder or more than £1000, whichever is the greater. Costs above this level are irrecoverable (except, sometimes, when the works are urgent) unless the freeholder has taken steps to inform and consult tenants. If the leaseholders are not represented by a recognised tenants' association (for which see below) these steps are as follows:

Estimates At least two estimates must be obtained, of which at least one must be from someone wholly unconnected with the freeholder (obviously a building firm that the freeholder owns or works for is not 'wholly unconnected'; nor is the freeholder's managing agent).

Notification to leaseholders The freeholder must either display a copy of the estimates somewhere they are likely to be seen by everyone liable to pay the service charge, or (preferably) send copies to everyone liable to pay the service charge.

Consultation The notification must describe the works to be carried out and must seek comments and observations, giving a deadline for replies and an address in the UK to which they may be sent. The deadline must be at least a month after the notice was sent or displayed.

Freeholder's response The freeholder must 'have regard' to any representations received. This does not mean, of course, that the freeholder must do what the leaseholders say. It does mean, however, that the freeholder must consider any comments received, and good freeholders often demonstrate that they have done so by sending a reasoned reply.

27

THE LEASEHOLDERS HANDBOOK

If a service charge is challenged in court for failure to follow these procedures, it is a defence for the freeholder to show that the works were urgent. However, the court would need to be satisfied that the urgency was genuine and that the freeholder behaved reasonably in the circumstances.

Section 20 is important because it gives the leaseholders notification of any unusual items in the offing and gives them an opportunity to raise any concerns and objections. If the leaseholder has any reservations at all, it is vital that they be put before the freeholder at this stage. It is highly unlikely, in the event of legal action later, that the court will support a leaseholder who raised no objection until the bill arrived.

It is common for freeholders and their agents to fail to comply with the requirements of section 20. This comment applies not only where the freehold is owned by an individual or a relatively small organisation (where mistakes might be more understandable) but also where the freeholder is a large, well resourced body like a local authority. As a result leaseholders are often paying service charges that are not due, so all leaseholders should, before paying a service charge containing unusual items, ensure that section 20, if it applies, has been scrupulously followed. If not, they can refuse to pay.

Other Protection for Leaseholders

Grant-aided works: If the freeholder has received a grant towards the cost of carrying out the works, the amount must be deducted from the service charge levied on leaseholders.

Late charging: Service charge bills may not normally include costs incurred more than eighteen months earlier. The freeholder may, however, notify leaseholders within the eighteen month period that they will have to pay a certain cost, and then bill them later. This might happen if, for instance, the freeholder is in dispute with a contractor about the level of a bill or the standard of work.

Pre-charging: Sometimes a lease will contain a provision allowing the freeholder to make a charge to cover future costs besides those already incurred. This practice, which is perfectly lawful in itself, may be in the interests of the leaseholders by spreading over a longer period the cost of major works. It is, however, subject to the same requirement of reasonableness.

Court costs: Section 20C provides protection against a specific abuse of the service charge system by freeholders. Previously, freeholders tended to regard their legal costs as part of the process of managing the housing and thus as recoverable from leaseholders. Such an attitude is not necessarily unreasonable: if, for instance, the freeholder is suing a builder for poor work, he is, in effect, acting on behalf of all the leaseholders and it is fair that they should pay any legal costs. But suppose the freeholder were involved in legal proceedings against one of the leaseholders: if the leaseholder lost, he would probably be ordered to pay the freeholder's costs as well as his own; but if the freeholder lost, and had to pay both his own and the leaseholder's costs, he could simply, under the previous law, recover the money as part of the management element in the service charge. This meant that the freeholder was able to pursue legal action against leaseholders without fear of heavy legal costs in the event of defeat, the very factor that deters most people from resorting to law. To prevent this, section 20C allows leaseholders to seek an order that the freeholder's legal costs must not be counted towards service charges. Such an order is available in respect of not only court proceedings but also proceedings before a Leasehold Valuation Tribunal, the Lands Tribunal, or an arbitral tribunal. An application for an order may be made by the leaseholder concerned in the case to the court or tribunal hearing it. If the case has finished, any leaseholder may apply for an order to the Lands Tribunal if the case was heard there, to any Leasehold Valuation Tribunal if it was heard by a LVT, or otherwise to the county court.

Service charges held on trust: Section 42 of the Landlord and Tenant Act 1987 further strengthened the position of leaseholders by laying down that the freeholder, or the freeholder's agent, must hold service charge monies in a suitable trust fund that will ensure that the money is protected and cannot be seized by the freeholder's creditors if the freeholder goes bankrupt or into liquidation. However, public sector freeholders, notably local authorities and registered housing associations, are exempt from this requirement.

Insurance: Usually, any insurance required under the lease will be taken out by the freeholder and this is discussed below. Occasionally, however, the leaseholder will be required to take out insurance with a company nominated by the freeholder. If the leaseholder thinks he is getting a poor deal, he can apply to the county court or a Leasehold Valuation Tribunal which, if satisfied that the insurance is unsatisfactory or the premiums are unreasonably high, can order the freeholder to nominate another insurer.

'Period of Grace': When a dwelling is sold under the right to buy by a local authority or non-charitable housing association, the purchaser is given an estimate of service charges for the following five years. This estimate is the maximum recoverable during that time. Some purchasers under the right to buy have, however, had a very rude shock when the five year period of grace expires - see *Exceptionally High Service Charges* below.

The role of a recognised tenants' association
The tenants who are liable to pay for the provision of services may, if they wish, form a recognised tenants' association (RTA) under section 29 of the Landlord and Tenant Act 1985. Note that leaseholders count as tenants for this purpose (see Chapter One, where it explained that legally the two terms are interchangeable). If the freeholder refuses to give a notice recognising the RTA, it may

apply for recognition to any member of the local Rent Assessment Committee panel ('Rent Assessment Committee' is the official term for a Leasehold Valuation Tribunal when it is carrying out certain functions, not otherwise relevant to leaseholders, under the Rent Act 1977).

An important benefit of having a RTA is that it has the right, at the beginning of the consultation process, to recommend persons or organisations that should be invited to submit estimates. However, the freeholder is under no obligation to accept these recommendations.

Another advantage is that the RTA can, whether the freeholder likes it or not, appoint a qualified surveyor to advise on matters relating to service charges. The surveyor has extensive rights to inspect the freeholder's documentation and take copies, and can enforce these rights in court if necessary.

Challenging Service Charges

The Landlord and Tenant Act not only allows leaseholders to take action against unreasonable behaviour by the freeholder; it also enables them to take the initiative. This is done in two ways: by giving leaseholders rights to demand information, and by allowing them to challenge the reasonableness of the charge.

Right to require information

Leaseholders have the right to ask freeholders for a written summary of costs counting towards the service charge. Such a summary must cover either the twelve months up to the point where it was requested or, if accounts are drawn up annually, the last complete twelve-month accounting period before the request was made. It must be sent to the leaseholder within one month of the request or within six months of the end of the period it covers, whichever is the later. Failure to provide it without reasonable excuse is a criminal offence carrying a maximum fine of £2500.

The law lays down some minimum requirements for the summary. It must:

- cover all the costs incurred during the twelve months it covers, even if they were included in service charge bills of an earlier or later period (see above for late charging and pre-charging);
- show how the costs incurred by the freeholder are reflected in the service charges paid, or to be paid, by leaseholders;
- say whether it includes any work covered by a grant (see above);
- distinguish: (a) those costs incurred for which the freeholder was not billed during the period; (b) those for which he was billed and did not pay; (c) those for which he paid bills.

If it covers five or more dwellings, the summary must, in addition, be certified by a qualified accountant as being a fair summary, complying with the Act, and supported by appropriate documentation.

The purpose of section 22 is to put leaseholders in a position to challenge their service charges. After receiving the summary, the leaseholder has six months in which to ask the freeholder to make facilities available so that he can inspect the documents supporting the summary (bills, receipts, and so on) and take copies or extracts. The freeholder must respond within a month and make the facilities available within the two months following that; the inspection itself must be free, although the freeholder can make a reasonable charge for the copies and extracts. Failure to provide these facilities, like failure to supply the summary, is punishable by a fine of up to £2500.

Very similar rules apply where the lease allows, or requires, the freeholder to take out insurance against certain contingencies, such as major repair, and to recover the premiums through the service charge. This is not unreasonable in itself and will, indeed, often be in the interests of leaseholders. The danger is, however, that the freeholder, knowing that the premiums are, in effect, being paid by someone else, has no incentive to shop around for the best deal.

Section 30A of the Landlord and Tenant Act 1985 therefore lays down that leaseholders, or the secretary of the recognised tenants' association if there is one, may ask the freeholder for information about the policy. Failure to supply it, or to make facilities to inspect relevant documents available if requested to do so, is an offence incurring a fine of up to £2500.

It must be acknowledged that the rules allowing leaseholders to require information about service charges are, particularly in view of the £2500 fines, fairly onerous from the freeholder's point of view.

It is the purpose of this book to inform leaseholders of their rights, not to make life difficult for freeholders: nevertheless, it must be admitted that if leaseholders wish to pursue a policy of confronting freeholders, and to cause them as much trouble as possible, sections 21, 22, and 30A offer plenty of scope.

Challenging the reasonableness of a service charge
Any leaseholder liable to pay a service charge, and for that matter any freeholder levying one, may refer the charge to a Leasehold Valuation Tribunal to determine its reasonableness. This may be done at any time, even when the service in question is merely a proposal by the freeholder (for instance, for future major works). But the LVT will not consider a service charge if:

-    it has already been approved by a court; or
-    if the leaseholder has agreed to refer it to arbitration; or
-    if the leaseholder has agreed it.

The first of these exceptions is obvious and the second is unlikely to apply very often. The third one is the problem: leaseholders should be careful, in their dealings with freeholders, to say or do nothing that could be taken to imply that they agree with any service charge that is in any way doubtful.

The LVT will consider:
-   whether the freeholder's costs of services, repairs, maintenance, insurance, or management are reasonably incurred;
-   whether the services or works are of a reasonable standard; and
-   whether any payment required in advance is reasonable.

The fees for application to a LVT can be obtained from the LVT and will usually change annually. Appeal against a LVT decision is not to the courts but to the Lands Tribunal.

By section 19 of the Landlord and Tenant Act 1985, any service charge deemed unreasonable by the LVT is irrecoverable by the freeholder. The determination of service charges by the LVT also plays an important part in the rules governing the use of forfeiture to recover service charges. .

Forfeiture for Unpaid Service Charges
Forfeiture was mentioned at the end of Chapter Two. Briefly, it is the right of the freeholder to take possession of the property if the leaseholder breaches the lease.

By section 81 of the Housing Act 1996, forfeiture for an unpaid service charge is available to the freeholder only if:

-   the leaseholder has agreed the charge; or
-   the charge has been upheld through arbitration or by a court.

Regarding the first of these, it is necessary only to reiterate the warning to leaseholders to say or do nothing that could possibly be construed as representing their agreement to any service charge about whose legitimacy they have the slightest doubt.

Regarding the second, it should be noted that where the leaseholder has not agreed the service charge, court proceedings or formal arbitration are necessary before the freeholder can forfeit the lease. The freeholder can still begin the process by issuing a section

146 notice (see Chapter Two) but it must state that the forfeiture cannot proceed until the requirements of section 81 have been met.

If proceedings in court depend on the reasonableness or otherwise of a service charge, the court has the power to decide the matter itself or refer it to a LVT; if it takes the latter option, the LVT's decision will have the force of a court order and if it upholds the service charge the freeholder can go ahead and seek forfeiture (although the leaseholder will still be able to challenge the forfeiture in court). But this applies only where the LVT is used as part of court proceedings; where the view of the LVT is sought independently of court proceedings, it will not in itself permit forfeiture.

Once the leaseholder has agreed the service charge or it has been upheld in court or through arbitration, forfeiture becomes a serious threat and in this situation the advice can only be to pay the charge if at all possible. If, however, the leaseholder is unable to pay he may find it helpful to contact his mortgagee (if any). For the mortgagee, forfeiture is a disaster because it is likely to be left with a large unsecured debt on its hands, so many mortgagees in this situation will pay the service charges and add the cost to the outstanding mortgage. This does not solve the leaseholder's long term problem - that his lease commits him to payments he is unable to meet - but it will give him a little breathing space and may enable him to sell up and pay off his debts.

Exceptionally High Service Charges

So far this Chapter has focused on service charges of normal proportions that, however unforeseen and unwelcome they may be, should be within the means of the great majority of leaseholders. A minority of leaseholders, however, face the much more serious problem of consistently very high service charges. Where the cause is sharp practice by the freeholder, or failure to observe the legal requirements, the leaseholder can look for protection to the Landlord and Tenant Act as described above. Often, however, the freeholder is not to blame: rather, the problem is that the work is genuinely necessary and unavoidably expensive. In this situation, and provided the landlord carefully follows the procedures laid down, the Landlord and Tenant Act offers no protection.

In what sort of housing is this most likely to occur? It is more likely to affect flats than houses because flats tend to contain potentially very expensive components such as lifts or communal arrangements for heating or ventilation. They are also more likely to have been built using construction methods or designs in vogue at one time but since found to lead to serious maintenance problems and high costs, whereas house building seems to be innately conservative and resistant to innovation: for instance, many blocks of flats contain asbestos, but very few houses. All these problems apply to flats in general, but there is an additional problem with blocks of flats owned by local authorities and housing associations: namely that, unlike blocks of flats developed by commercial owners for sale, they are likely to combine rented properties, let to periodic tenants in the usual way, with leasehold properties, sold at some point in the past under the right to buy or some similar scheme. These 'mixed managed' blocks present special problems for both categories of resident as well as the freeholder.

Clearly, there is no satisfactory way to resolve this problem. In a privately developed block, occupied wholly by leaseholders, the freeholder might possibly be prevailed upon to delay the repairs for a time if the leaseholders are prepared to put up with the poor conditions; but the Council can hardly be expected to take the same view when most of the residents are periodic tenants. Both the Council and the periodic tenants are likely to argue that the leaseholders are being asked to do no more than they agreed to do when they bought their leases.

All this book can do is warn prospective leaseholders of the serious problems that can arise in a minority of cases, and suggest some of the questions that they should ask before signing the lease.

What is the condition of the building as a whole? No one would buy a house, or an individual flat, without looking closely at its condition and estimating how much money it may need to have spent on it. But, when a flat is being bought, whether it is purpose-built or a conversion, it is equally important to look at the entire building of which it forms a part. The vendor should be asked for copies of past service charges, the freeholder should be asked whether major work is likely in the foreseeable future and what it is likely to cost, and an independent surveyor should be asked to report.

What is the leaseholder's liability? The lease will specify what the leaseholder must pay for. Sometimes it will require him to contribute to things from which he does not benefit. For example, it is common for even ground floor leaseholders to be expected to contribute to the costs of the lifts; and some leaseholders, having paid out of their own pockets to replace their windows, are outraged to discover, when the freeholder has the windows of the whole block renewed, that they are required to pay a share of the cost.

Provisions such as these are much resented by many leaseholders, who argue that they are unfair; but the time to object to such unfairness is before signing the lease, not many years later when the bills come in. It is therefore essential that anyone proposing to enter into a lease should first consult a solicitor.

Is there a 'period of grace' or other safeguard? Right to buy leases contain an estimate of service charges for five years following the sale and that is the maximum that the Council may charge. Many purchasers, reassured by this, have signed the lease without paying much attention to the likely level of service charges thereafter, expecting perhaps to have sold at a profit and moved on before the five years expire. If so, they have been reminded of what many people forgot during the 1980s: that property prices can go down as well as up. In short, it is unwise to rely on a 'period of grace' to provide anything other than short-term relief; and in particular it is unwise to speculate on the future behaviour of the housing market.

What are the prospects for resale? Traditionally, the homeowner's last resort in the face of overwhelming financial problems is to sell up in the expectation that the proceeds will suffice to pay off the mortgage, settle other outstanding debts such as service charges, and still leave something over. A stagnant property market has upset many calculations of this kind, but selling up remains an option if the mortgage is appreciably less than the value of the property, and if the service charges are not too high. So it is important to assess the saleability of the dwelling by asking whether future purchasers are likely to be put off by anything about the flat itself or the block and district to which it belongs, and above all whether mortgage lenders are likely to look on it favourably.

4

PURCHASING THE FREEHOLD AND EXTENSION OF LEASES

It has always been, and still is, open to the freeholder and the leaseholder to negotiate different arrangements other than the automatic expiry of a lease at the end of its term.

The freeholder might agree to sell the freehold to the leaseholder. The sale of the freehold to the leaseholder is called 'enfranchisement' of the lease, because it is freed, or 'enfranchised', from the overriding freehold, and replaces it. A further possibility is that the freeholder and leaseholder may agree to extend the lease beyond its original term. If agreements of this kind are negotiated, it is entirely for the freeholder and leaseholder to settle the conditions and the price.

In recent years, however, the law has forced freeholders, in certain circumstances, to sell freeholds or extend leases, whether they wish to or not. This has been done by three pieces of legislation: the Leasehold Reform Act 1967, the Landlord and Tenant Act 1987, and the Leasehold Reform, Housing and Urban Development Act 1993 (although all three Acts have been amended by later legislation, particularly the Housing Act 1996 and the Commonhold and Leasehold Reform Act 2002.). But before looking at the legislation, it is important to establish why extension and enfranchisement are important to the average leaseholder.

Extension of a Lease Some enlightened freeholders automatically extend the lease whenever it is assigned, so that if a lease that was originally granted for 125 years is assigned after 30, the assignee gets a lease not for 95 years, as one might expect, but for 125. From the leaseholder's point of view, such an arrangement is extremely valuable because otherwise the lease represents a wasting asset, whose valuable because otherwise the lease represents a wasting asset, whose value will drop sharply as the end of the term approaches. The arrangement can also benefit the freeholder by making the lease more valuable at the time of its original sale. But most leases are unaffected by assignment and would expire on the originally determined date were it not for legislation that obliges freeholders, in certain circumstances, to grant a fresh leas, of 90 years over and above the existing term to the leaseholder: this is described below.

Individual Enfranchisement of a Lease Legislation, described below, now allows the leaseholder to acquire the freehold, in certain circumstances, whether or not the freeholder agrees. If not for this, the leaseholder would find that his home had reverted to the ownership of the freeholder at the end the lease and he would have to buy it back (assuming the freeholder were willing to sell). The freeholder is, however, entitled to compensation.

Collective Enfranchisement of Leases The problem with leasehold enfranchisement is that the property concerned must be capable of being held on a freehold basis. Where it stands on a distinct and definable piece of land this does not present a problem: the freehold of the land is transferred to the leaseholder and, as explained in Section One, any buildings on it are automatically transferred too. But if the property is only part of a larger building, it may not be attached to its own unique piece of land in the same way, so individual enfranchisement is not available to flat owners. If they wish to enfranchise, therefore, they have to agree among themselves that a single person or body will buy the freehold on behalf of all of them, while they continue to hold leases of their individual flats. This is called 'collective enfranchisement', although this term is misleading because technically the leases have not been enfranchised at all: all that has happened is a change from the original freeholder to a new one nominated by the leaseholders.

Rights to Enfranchise and Extend Leases: General Principles

The Acts are available to what they describe as 'qualifying tenants': but the exact meaning of the term varies depending which right is being exercised under which Act. Usually, but not always, the term is defined in a way that excludes ordinary tenants and confines it to leaseholders. The definitions generally rely upon the concepts of long lease, a 'low rent', a residence test, certain other exemptions. We now look at these requirements.

A Long Lease For most purposes under the Acts, the leaseholder must own a lease originally granted for at least 21 years. Note that this is the term when the lease was granted, not the period it still has to run, so that a 99 year lease granted in 1905 is still a long lease in 1998 even though it has only six years to go. Recent legislation has put an end to a number of devices formerly inserted into leases by freeholders in order to avoid having to extend or enfranchise leases. Some were bizarre: leases were made terminable on extraneous events, such as royal marriages or deaths, because the lease was not regarded as long if it depended on an event that could occur at any time. These evasions have been of no effect since the 1993 Act, which provides that leases containing them shall be treated as long leases.

The Housing Act 1996 has added two further categories of long lease, namely those originally granted for 35 years or more and those originally granted for 50 years or more. In certain circumstances, described below, these leases are excluded from the low rent test.

A 'Low Rent' Because the law does not recognise the familiar distinction between tenants and leaseholders (see Chapter One), the legislation must find a way of telling them apart if it wants to give rights to leaseholders but not to tenants. This is done by defining a 'low rent': the idea is that, because leaseholders normally pay only a notional ground rent, anyone whose annual rent is less than a certain amount is likely to be a leaseholder, not a tenant. What this amount is depends on the date when the lease was originally granted (not the date when the current leaseholder acquired it).

- If the lease was first granted before 1st April 1963, a 'low rent' is one that was, in the first year of the lease, less than two-thirds of the letting value of the property at that time. In almost all cases, leasehold ground rents will be so far below the letting value (the amount that could be got from an ordinary tenant) that there is unlikely to be any dispute about whether the rent qualifies as low. This is just as well, because such a dispute could be settled only by a professional valuer who would also have to be something of an historian, because he would be asked to give his opinion of the letting value not at the present day but many decades ago.

- If the lease was first granted between 1st April 1963 and 31st March 1990, the question is much simpler. A 'low rent' is one that was, in the first year of the lease, less than two-thirds of the rateable value of the dwelling at the time. This is easy to check: the local authority will have records of rateable values. In the rare cases where the property had no rateable value when first let, the low rent test operates for the first year a rateable value applied, not the first year of the lease.

- If the lease has been granted since 1st April 1990 (the date of the abolition of domestic rates), it is simpler still. The rent in the first year of the lease must have been £1000 or less in the City of London and the London Boroughs and £250 or less elsewhere in England and Wales.

However, the importance of the low rent test has been greatly diminished by the Commonhold and Leasehold Reform Act 2002, which abolishes it as a criteria for extending leases.

Residence Test Under the Commonhold and Leasehold Reform Act 2002, the residence test has been abolished for the extension of leases and enfranchisement.

- The Acts do not apply if the property is within the precincts of a cathedral or owned by the Crown (however, it is possible that the Crown authorities will agree to a voluntary extension or enfranchisement of the lease). Some properties owned by the National Trust are also exempt.
- Other exemptions apply not across the board but to particular types of transaction. These are covered as the various Acts are discussed below.

Leasehold Reform Act 1967 (as amended by the 2002 Commonhold and Leasehold Reform Act): Leases of Houses

The first legislation to deal with leasehold extension and enfranchisement was the Leasehold Reform Act 1967. This Act is still in force, but is not relevant to most residential leaseholders, who will get more benefit from later legislation. It can therefore be dealt with fairly briefly.

The Act relates only to residential leases of houses - not flats. With certain exceptions, a leaseholder qualifies to use it if he passes the residence test (replaced by the Commonhold and Leasehold Reform Act 2002 by a new requirement that leaseholders must have held their lease for at least two years before exercising the right to enfranchise or extend the lease). The other requirement is that the leaseholder has a leases originally granted for 35 years or more. The Act allows leaseholders to acquire the freehold of their homes, or, if they prefer, extend the lease for 50 years.

In addition, the new Act makes provision for the leaseholder to buy the freehold after the lease has been extended.

The usual exemptions (see above) apply to the 1967 Act. In addition, it does not apply to most shared ownership leases granted by housing associations. The Act was formerly limited to properties below a certain value but as far as enfranchisement is concerned this restriction was abolished by the Leasehold Reform, Housing and Urban Development Act 1993. The value ceiling still applies to lease extension under the 1967 Act, however; there are complicated rules about this, but in most circumstances they will be irrelevant because any leaseholder, given the choice, is likely to go for outright enfranchisement of the lease rather than a 50 year extension.

Most leaseholders qualifying to make use of the 1967 Act (as amended) have long since done so, because the benefits of owning the freehold outweigh the drawback of having to pay the freeholder the difference (usually not very great) between the freehold and leasehold value of the house.

Generally speaking, therefore, remaining leasehold houses will be those to which the Act does not apply, either because the freeholder is exempt or because the house is attached to other property.

The last point is an important limitation on the 1967 Act (as amended): if the land on which the house stands is shared by any other property not covered by the lease, however small it may be compared with the house, the Act cannot be used. It may, however, be possible for the leaseholder of such a house to use the new rights in the Leasehold Reform, Housing and Urban Development Act 1993.

The procedure for enfranchisement under the 1967 (as amended) Act is as follows.

- The leaseholder serves a notice on the freeholder stating that he wishes to claim the freehold (or extend the lease). This notice should give particulars of the property and the lease, and should make it clear that the leaseholder satisfies the residence test.

- Within two months, the freeholder must send a counter notice that either accepts the leaseholder's claim or gives reasons for rejecting it. The freeholder may ask the leaseholder for a deposit of £25 or thrice the annual ground rent, whichever is more, and for proof that he holds the lease and meets the residence test. The leaseholder has 14 days to produce the money and 21 days to produce the proof.

- If the freeholder does not submit a counter notice within two months, the leaseholder's claim is automatically accepted. If the freeholder's counter notice unfairly rejects the leaseholder's claim, the leaseholder may apply to the county court.

- Obviously, the freeholder is justified in rejecting the claim if the property does not come under the Act or if the leaseholder does not qualify. In addition, the freeholder may reject the claim if he acquired the house before 18th February 1966 and needs the house, on expiry of the lease, as a home for himself or a member of his family. He may also refuse to extend the lease (but not to enfranchise it) if he plans to redevelop the property.

- Once it has been established that the leaseholder may enfranchise, a price must be agreed; if this is not possible, it will be set by a leasehold valuation tribunal. The Act lays down that the price should be the value of the freehold if it were being sold willingly but on the assumption that the lease were continuing and would be renewable under the Act. In effect, this formula means that the leaseholder is obliged to pay for what he is acquiring (the freehold) but not for what he has already got (the lease).

- Once a price has been agreed, or set by tribunal, either the freeholder or the leaseholder has one month to serve a notice on the other requiring him to complete. The freeholder must convey the freehold as a fee simple absolute, or (as a non-lawyer would say) outright.

Landlord and Tenant Act 1987: First Refusal and Mismanagement

The Landlord and Tenant Act 1987 was chiefly concerned with enabling leaseholders to protect themselves against unreasonable service charges, and it made numerous amendments to tighten the rules originally laid down in the Landlord and Tenant Act 1985 (see Chapter Three).

In addition, it granted leaseholders the important right of first refusal if the freehold of their property is sold. It also allowed leaseholders to acquire the freehold if the property is being mismanaged: however, this right is little used because of the difficult procedures involved, and although it remains on the statute book it is likely to fall into complete disuse because the 1993 Act has now given leaseholders the same right without having to prove mismanagement.

First refusal

The right of first refusal was granted in order to stop the practice of selling freeholds, without any reference to the leaseholders or other occupiers, from one person or organisation to another so that leaseholders were often completely in the dark about who the ultimate freeholder was. The right of first refusal remains important because it is sometimes available when ordinary collective enfranchisement, under the 1993 Act, is not possible.

The 1987 Act says that if the freeholder intends to sell the freehold he must first offer it to the leaseholders and other qualifying tenants. There are, however, some exceptions: the Act does not apply if the freeholder is selling to a member of his family, or if he lives in the block himself; nor does it apply if the block is not chiefly residential.

In addition, virtually all public sector freeholders are excluded from the Act: this means local authorities, registered housing associations, and various other bodies. It is, however, unlikely that this sort of body will wish to sell its freehold.

But if none of these exceptions applies, and if the majority of qualifying tenants (including leaseholders) wish to buy, they must be given the opportunity to meet the freeholder's price. For the purpose of defining a 'majority' there can be only one qualifying tenant in respect of each flat: in other words, joint tenants (or joint leaseholders) have only one 'vote' between them, and must agree between themselves how it will be used.

'Qualifying tenants' are:

- tenants entitled to a Fair Rent under the 1977 Rent Act: that is, most tenants
- tenants of self-contained dwellings holding a tenancy originally granted on or before 14th January 1989, but excluding council tenants; and
- leaseholders, except for business leaseholders (the normal 21 year minimum does not apply).

If the qualifying tenants and freeholder cannot agree terms for the sale, the freeholder is able to sell to someone else. However, the qualifying tenants must be informed of this sale and, most importantly, of the price. They then have the right to buy the freehold from the new owner at whatever price he paid. This is designed to stop the original freeholder from asking the qualifying tenants for an excessive price that they are bound to reject, then selling to someone else at a lower price. Similarly, if the freeholder carries out a sale without informing the qualifying tenants, they have the right to buy from the new freeholder for the same price that he paid.

The procedure under the 1987 Act for the right of first refusal is as follows.

- The freeholder notifies all qualifying tenants of his desire to sell and of the price at which he is willing to do so (including any non-monetary element). The notice must state the proposed method of sale: for instance, by conveyance or by auction.
- The freeholder must give the qualifying tenants at least two months to respond; and, if they say they wish to buy, at least a further two months (28 days if the sale is to be by auction) to come up with a nominee purchaser to acquire the freehold on their behalf. This could conceivably be in an individual or an organisation that already exists, but is much more likely to be a company set up specially for the purpose by the qualifying tenants, and under their control.
- During this period, the landlord and the qualifying tenants may wish to take the opportunity to negotiate the price.
- If a majority of the qualifying tenants have put forward a nominee purchaser and agreed with the freeholder on a price, the freeholder may not sell to anyone else.
- If the qualifying tenants fail to put forward a nominee purchaser, or if a mutually acceptable price is not agreed, the freeholder has twelve months to sell to someone else in accordance with the original notice (by auction, if that was the method specified; and in any other case for a price not less than that originally offered to the qualifying tenants). If no sale has taken place within twelve months, the freeholder must start the procedure again from scratch if he wishes to sell.

Mismanagement: the right to manage and to enfranchise
As mentioned above, the 1987 Act is designed mainly to protect leaseholders against mismanagement and sharp practice by freeholders. It therefore gives them the power of collective

enfranchisement against a freeholder guilty of serious or repeated breach of his obligations. The power is available to long leaseholders; the residential test does not apply, but a leaseholder does not qualify to use this part of the Act if he owns long leases of three or more flats in the block.

Moreover, this part of the 1987 Act does not apply where the freeholder is the Crown or a public body such as a local authority or a registered housing association. Nor does it apply when the freeholder resides in the property himself. It is available only where two-thirds or more of the flats in the block are let on long leases, and in blocks of ten flats or fewer a higher proportion is required. The court can make an order transferring the freehold to the leaseholders' nominee only if a manager appointed (see Chapter Two) by a court or LVT has controlled the premises for at least two years, unless the leaseholders can show:

- that the freeholder is and is likely to remain in breach of his obligations under the lease; and
- that the mere appointment of a manager would be an inadequate remedy.

All these restrictions suggest that the Act envisages that enfranchisement on grounds of mismanagement is very much a last resort; indeed, it is necessary for the leaseholders to take their case to court and get permission before they can proceed. The right was seldom used and, although it remains available in theory, in practice it has been superseded by the 1993 Act, which gives most leaseholders the right of collective enfranchisement whatever the standard of management and with no need for a court order.

Nevertheless, it is just possible there is a body of leaseholders somewhere willing to use the 1987 Act rather than the 1993 Act. The procedures for collective enfranchisement following mismanagement are therefore briefly set out here, with a warning that the general recommendation to employ a solicitor applies with special emphasis if this route is chosen.

- At least two-thirds of the qualifying leaseholders must serve a preliminary notice informing the freeholder that they intend to go to court to acquire the freehold. The notice must give the names and addresses of the leaseholder and the grounds for their application; the freeholder should also be given a reasonable deadline to rectify the problems if it is possible for him to do so.
- The leaseholders must apply to the court, giving their reasons for dissatisfaction and requesting an order to transfer the freehold to their nominee purchaser (probably, as with other forms of collective enfranchisement, a company set up for the purpose).
- If satisfied that it is fair to do so, the court will transfer the block to the nominee purchaser. The price will have to be agreed by the leaseholders and the freeholder; or, if (as is likely) this is not possible, by a Leasehold Valuation Tribunal. The price will be the value of the freehold on the assumption that all the leases are to continue: there will be no additional 'marriage value' (see below), and this is one of the few reasons for preferring to use the 1987 Act rather than the 1993 Act.

Leasehold Reform, Housing and Urban Development Act 1993 (as amended by the Commonhold and Leasehold reform Act 2002): Collective Enfranchisement and Lease Extension

The 1993 Act greatly extended the rights of leaseholders It made a number of adjustments, dealt with above, to existing rights under the 1967 and 1987 Acts; in addition, it created two new rights for leaseholders of flats. These are the right to collective enfranchisement, and the right to extend individual leases.

a: Collective enfranchisement under the 1993 Act (as amended)
In outline, the right to collective enfranchisement under the 1993 Act

is similar to, but much easier than, collective enfranchisement under the 1987 Act. Under both schemes, qualifying leaseholders nominate a purchaser to whom the freeholder can be forced to sell; but under the 1993 Act there is no need for a court order and no need to show that there has been mismanagement.

The 1993 Act is available to long leaseholders provided that at least two-thirds of the flats in the block are let on long leases and that at least half of the leaseholders involved in the enfranchisement satisfy the test of holding a lease for at least two years prior to the application.

Between them, the leaseholders involved must also occupy at least half of the total number of flats in the block.

However, the block may not be enfranchised if it falls within the normal exemptions, or if it is not chiefly residential, or if it is a house converted into four flats or fewer and the freeholder or a member of his family lives in one of them. Even if there is a resident freeholder, however, the scheme applies to houses converted into five flats or more and to purpose-built blocks even if they contain only two flats.

There are special provisions for any parts of the building that are occupied by people or organisations other than qualifying leaseholders. Some flats may be let to periodic tenants, for instance, and a block that faces a main road may well contain shop units on the ground floor. Any such parts may, and in some cases must, be leased back to the original freeholder when the block is acquired. 'Leaseback', as it is called, is mandatory for any flats let to periodic tenants (secure or assured) by a local authority or a registered housing association. This means that they can continue as council (or association) tenants, and do not lose any legal rights. It is up to the freeholder (not the leaseholders) whether he wants a leaseback of other flats or premises, such as business units or flats occupied by non-qualifying leaseholders. Unless the parties agree otherwise, leaseback is for 999 years at a notional rent.

The leaseholders must nominate a purchaser. This could be an individual - one of the leaseholders, perhaps, if he has the confidence of the others and is willing to undertake the role. Or there may be some existing organisation that the leaseholders wish to have as their new freeholder.

Another possibility is that two, three, or four individuals could purchase jointly - but no more than four, because under the Law of Property Act 1925 it is not possible for more than four individuals to share an estate in land such as a freehold. In most cases, however, the leaseholders will wish to own the freehold jointly and if there are more than four of them the way to achieve this is to form a corporate body in which all of them own shares. Such a body will probably be registered as a company, but it could be a society under the Industrial and Provident Societies Act 1965. See chapter 6 for advice on how to set up a flat management company.

The cost of setting up a company or society is only part of the expense in which collective enfranchisement will involve leaseholders. They will also have to pay both their own and the freeholder's legal and professional costs.

Above all, they must pay the purchase price of the freehold, which, unless they come to an agreement with the freeholder, will be decided by a leasehold valuation tribunal in accordance with rules laid down in the Act. These say that the price consists of two components: the open market value and the 'marriage value'.

According to the formula in the Act, the **open market value** should reflect the income the freeholder would have received from rents plus the prospect of regaining possession of the parts of the building currently let.

The other component in the price, the **'marriage value'**, is based on the assumption that, combined (as they will be after enfranchisement), the leases and the freehold have a greater value than they would if sold separately. The Act says the freeholder is entitled to at least half this amount. In most cases, however, especially where the leases have a long time to run, the marriage value will be low.

Altogether the costs of enfranchisement may be considerable. It is therefore prudent for leaseholders to explore the ground before committing themselves. This can be done by any qualifying leaseholder by serving a notice on the freeholder (or whomever the leaseholder pays rent to) under section 11 of the Act. Such a notice obliges the freeholder to disclose, within 28 days, information that will be relevant to any sale, such as title deeds, surveyor's reports, planning restrictions, and so on. This will allow the leaseholders to take an informed view of whether they wish to go for collective enfranchisement and, if so, on what terms. At this stage, they should take their time and think it over carefully, for if they proceed further they will be obliged to pay the freeholder's legal costs if they later decide to withdraw.

It may be appropriate, too, at this stage, for the leaseholders to ask the freeholder whether he is prepared to consider a voluntary sale without forcing all concerned to go through the somewhat elaborate procedures laid down by the 1993 Act. A reasonable freeholder, since he will be aware that he can be forced to sell anyway, may well be willing to discuss this.

If the leaseholders decide to go ahead with collective enfranchisement under the 1993 Act, the procedure is:

- The leaseholders commission a surveyor to carry out a valuation according to the principles laid down in the Act.
- The leaseholders serve an initial notice (also called a 'section 13 notice') giving the names and addresses of the leaseholders involved and of the nominee purchaser, particulars of their leases to show that the qualify under the Act, and exactly specifying what property they wish to enfranchise and which parts, if any, they will lease back. The notice must also propose a price, and give the freeholder at least two months to reply. Once the initial notice has been served, the freeholder may not sell the freehold to

any third party.

- From now on, the nominee purchaser handles proceedings on behalf of the leaseholders. The freeholder may require the nominee purchaser to provide evidence to show that the participating leaseholders are qualified under the Act. If the nominee purchaser does not respond within 21 days, the freeholder may in some circumstances treat the initial notice as being withdrawn.

- By the date specified in the initial notice, the freeholder must serve a counter notice either accepting the leaseholders' right to enfranchise or giving reasons for rejecting it. The freeholder must also state whether he accepts the details of the leaseholders' proposal as regards price and exactly what is to be included in the sale, and must say whether he wishes to lease back any parts of the property (in addition to those where leaseback is mandatory). The freeholder may refuse to exercise his right to lease back parts of the premises let on lucrative business lets because the effect of this will be to increase the price and, perhaps, deter the leaseholders from continuing. In the unlikely event that most of the leaseholders' leases have less than five years to run, the freeholder has the right to stop the enfranchisement if he can satisfy a court that he intends to redevelop the block.

- The intention of the Act is that after the freeholder's counter notice the parties will attempt to resolve any differences, so that the sale of the freehold can proceed on agreed terms. Often, however, agreement will be impossible and in that case the matters in dispute are referred to a Leasehold Valuation Tribunal. Such a referral must take place at least two months, and not more than six months, after the freeholder's counter notice; if no agreement is reached, and no referral made, after six months, the initial notice will be deemed withdrawn.

- Once the terms have been settled, the parties have two months to exchange contracts. At the end of this time, the nominee purchaser has a further two months to ask a court to transfer the freehold on the terms agreed (or determined by the tribunal); or the freeholder may ask the court to rule that the initial notice shall be treated as being withdrawn.

- If for any reason the sale does not go ahead, the leaseholders must wait at least a year before serving another preliminary notice.

b: Lease extension under the 1993 Act (as amended)

Although the right to collective enfranchisement, as created by the 1993 Act, is of great importance because it makes a fundamental shift in the relationship between freeholders and leaseholders, the complex procedures mean that it is likely to be relatively seldom used. On the other hand, the right to a new lease, which was also created (for flat owners) by the 1993 Act (as amended), is likely to prove of immense practical benefit to thousands of leaseholders, not least because it can be exercised on an individual basis.

The leaseholder will have to pay the freeholder a sum consisting of two components calculated in accordance with rules set out in the Act. The first represents the reduction in the market value of the freehold that results because the freeholder will now have to wait to regain possession for 90 years longer than would otherwise have been the case. The less time the old lease had to run, the higher this component is likely to be. The second component is the 'marriage value', reflecting the higher value of a longer lease. As with collective enfranchisement, the freeholder is entitled to at least 50% of the marriage value.

A leaseholder who is contemplating a lease extension should begin by serving a preliminary notice on the freeholder. This has the same function as with collective enfranchisement: it commits the leaseholder to nothing, but requires the freeholder to supply within 28 days the information that will enable the leaseholder to decide whether to go ahead.

- The leaseholder serves an initial notice (a 'section 42 notice') on the freeholder. This must give details of the property concerned as well as of the leaseholder and his claim to qualify to use the 1993 Act. It must state how much the leaseholder proposes to pay, and set a date, at least two months ahead, by which the freeholder must reply. Once the notice has been served, the leaseholder must allow the freeholder to have access to the flat for the purpose of valuation.

- The freeholder must either agree that the leaseholder qualifies under the Act, or give reasons for disagreeing. If the freeholder agrees that the leaseholder is qualified to extend the lease, he may still suggest that the price of the new lease, or its other terms, should be different to the leaseholder's proposals. The freeholder can go to court for permission to reject the extension entirely if the current lease has less than five years to run and the freeholder then intends to redevelop the property.

  - The freeholder and leaseholder should then attempt to resolve any differences by negotiation. If agreement is not reached, the question may be referred to the Leasehold Valuation Tribunal at lease two months, and not less than six months, after the freeholder's counter notice. If, six months after the counter notice, there is neither an agreement nor a referral to a tribunal, the leaseholder's initial notice will be deemed withdrawn. In this event the leaseholder is liable for any reasonable expenses incurred by the freeholder.

- Once the terms are settled, either by negotiation or by the tribunal, the parties have two months to exchange contracts. If exchange does not take place during this period, the leaseholder has a further two months to apply to court for an order extending the lease on the terms agreed (or laid down by a tribunal).

It should be noted that collective enfranchisement takes priority over individual lease extensions, so that the effect of an initial notice of collective enfranchisement is to freeze, for the time being, any current claims to extend leases. If the collective enfranchisement fails to go ahead, the extension claims resume where they left off.

5.

THE COMMONHOLD AND LEASEHOLD REFORM ACT 2002

The Commonhold and Leasehold Reform Act became law in May 2002, and will be implemented in stages. Part 1 of the bill introduces a new form of tenure called commonhold. Commonhold is applicable to new developments but is not compulsory. Existing blocks of flats can also convert to commonhold voluntarily if all leaseholders agree. Commonhold essentially means that a company (commonhold association), with each commonholder having a share, is formed. Individual flats are freehold and the common parts are owned and managed collectively. A commonhold association will have a commonhold community statement which is a statement defining how the commonhold will be managed.

The Act provides details about commonhold and the management of commonhold flats. These cover accounting and budgeting and also details about commonhold associations plus other elements. For more details about the new form of tenure you should visit www.housing.dtlr.gov.uk.

Part two of the Act introduces a new no-fault right to manage, which will enable leaseholders to take over the management of their building without having to prove fault on the part of the landlord or pay him or her any compensation. Enfranchisement (collective purchase of the freehold) is made easier for leaseholders of flats and houses. Lease extensions are easier to obtain. Leaseholders of houses who previously extended their leases can now buy the freehold. The rights of those who have inherited a leasehold house are improved, leaseholders rights against unreasonable service charges are strengthened, and accounting rules are strengthened. In addition, lease variations are easier to obtain, the right to seek appointment of a new manager is strengthened, landlords must now demand ground rent in writing before they can collect and the roles of Leasehold Valuation Tribunals are consolidated and strengthened.

The Right to Manage

Although long leaseholders of flats have purchased the right to live in their property, control of the management, maintenance and insurance of the property normally remains in the hands of the landlord. Leaseholders are normally obliged under their leases to meet the full costs of the landlords functions, but enjoy little control over the quality and value for money of these services.

In order to counter this, the new Act has introduced the 'no fault' right to manage. The Act provides that:

- leaseholders will be able to collectively take over the management duties for the building, for example leaseholders will be able to have a greater degree of control over the level and cost of services and appoint their own choice of managing agents and select their own insurers
- leaseholders will not have to prove any fault or shortcomings on the part of the landlord in order to exercise the right
- leaseholders will not be required to pay any compensation to the landlord for exercising the right.

Qualifying requirements

The eligibility requirements will ensure that neither a minority of qualifying tenants, nor a minority of the residents in a block, could take control. The eligibility requirements are as follows:

- Leaseholders must own a long lease (more than 21 years)
- Where the lease is a shred ownership lease, the leaseholder would have to hold a 100% share of the equity
- Leaseholders must become members of a company which is

properly constituted for the purposes of collective management – that will be a private company limited by guarantee (see chapter six) which must include the exercise of the right to manage as one of its main objects.

- At least two thirds of the flats in the building would have to be held by long leaseholders, and the participating leaseholders would have to hold the leases of at least half of the flats in the blocks.
- RTM will apply to any premises containing two or more flats held by qualifying tenants. This includes both a self-contained building and a vertically separated part of the building (for example a converted terraced house)
- Premises would also include any associated parts, such as garages and gardens, which are for the sole use of the residents of the block in question.

Exclusions
The following are excluded from the RTM:

- Properties in mixed residential and non-residential use where the internal floor are of the non-residential parts exceeds 25% of the total internal floor area of the property.
- Any premises which have been converted into flats (or a mixture of flats and other units used as dwellings e.g. bedsits) if the converted building contains no more than four units and the landlord (or an adult member of the family) lives in one of these units and has done so for the previous twelve months.
- Any premises where the landlord is a local authority. Local authority tenants already have a separate right to manage.
- Where an RTM management body loses the management of a property for any reason. In such circumstances the block in question will be excluded from any exercise of RTM for four years from the date that the body ceased their management duties,

unless the permission of a Leasehold Valuation Tribunal is obtained.

Almost certainly, if leaseholders chose to go down this road, then the appointment of a Chartered Surveyor or Lawyer would be necessary to guide the process through.

Lease renewals for flats

The right for leaseholders to acquire a new lease for their property, which adds on 90 years over and above the existing term, is an individual right arising out of the 1993 Leasehold, Housing and Urban Development Act. The existing regime is modified as follows:

- removes the low rent test
- abolishes the residence test, which will benefit leaseholders who occupy their flat as a second home or sub-let it. However, a tenant must have been a leaseholder for two years prior to the application to extend the lease
- provides that any marriage value (increase in value by extending) be shared equally between landlord and leaseholder; and to presume that there is no marriage value where the lease runs for over 80 years.
- Helps representatives of deceased leaseholders by allowing them to qualify for the right where the deceased qualified immediately before they died. The right would be exercisable for a period of six months starting from the date of the grant of probate or letters of administration.

Enfranchisement

The new Act includes a number of changes to the collective enfranchisement provisions in Chapter 1 of Part 1 of the Leasehold Reform, Housing and Urban Development Act 1993.

Existing rules

- To be eligible leaseholders must be qualifying tenants, which means that leaseholders must hold a lease which when originally granted was for a period of more than 21 years. This does not include a business lease.
- The lease must also be at a low rent-there is a complex test for this, unless it is for a particularly low term (over 35 years).
- The building must include at least two flats occupied by qualifying tenants. At least two thirds of all the flats in the building must be occupied by qualifying tenants.
- Any non-domestic component in the block must not exceed 10% of the floor area.
- The building does not qualify if it is a converted property of four or fewer flats and a resident landlord or a member of their family is living in one of them
- The group of qualifying tenants seeking to enfranchise must include at least two thirds of all the qualifying tenants in the block
- At least half the residents must satisfy the residence test, that is, they must have occupied the flat for the last 12 months or for periods adding up to three out of the last ten years.

Revised eligibility criteria in the new Act

- Abolition of the residence test
- For individual leaseholders the low rent test will be abolished
- The resident landlord exemption would be restricted to cases where the resident landlord had carried out the conversion
- The requirement to include at least two thirds of the qualifying tenants in the block is removed but the group would continue to have to hold the leases of at least half of the flats in the block

- The threshold for the non domestic component is raised to 25%
- Participating leaseholders must be members of a company which is properly constituted for the purposes of ownership and management
- All qualifying leaseholders have the right to participate in the enfranchisement process by becoming members of the company.

Valuation

The 1993 Act sets down certain valuation rules and principles which must be followed in calculating the price payable for the freehold. In outline, the price payable is an aggregate of three components:

- the open market value of the freeholders interest in the premises
- The freeholders share of the 'marriage value'
- Any compensation for losses.

The freeholder is also entitled to recover his or her reasonable costs of dealing with the enfranchisement, other than the costs associated with appearing before a LVT.

Revised changes to valuation

The new Act introduces the following measures:

- to share the marriage value equally between landlord and leaseholder
- to presume that there is no marriage value where the leases of all participating leaseholders have more than 80 years to run
- to remove the unfettered right of appeal to the Lands Tribunal against leasehold valuation (LVT) decisions, so that permission would need to be sought from the LVT or Lands Tribunal.

Service charges and administration charges

The new Act introduces a number of changes to leaseholders rights in relation to service charges under the Landlord and Tenant Act 1985. Existing rights are:

- the right to be consulted about major works
- the right for service charges to be reasonable
- the right to challenge the reasonableness of any service charge or of the standard of work
- the right to certain information about service charges

The new Act will:

- require landlords to provide annual accounting statements that provide information about monies paid into a service charge fund, or standing to the credit of the service charge fund as well as costs incurred by the landlord. Leaseholders will be able to withhold service charges if this requirement has not been met
- require landlords to provide leaseholders with a summary of their rights and obligations in relation to service charges
- to give leaseholders the right to inspect documentation relevant to their accounting statements within 21 days of their request. Leaseholders will also be able to take copies of that information, or have copies provided to them on payment of a reasonable fee
- clarify that leaseholders can challenge service charges at a Leasehold Valuation Tribunal where the amount has already been paid to a landlord
- require landlords to hold service charges funds in a designated separate client account.
- Leaseholders will have the right to ask for proof that this requirement has been met

- provide that where leaseholders have reasonable grounds for believing that the landlord is not holding their service charges in a separate account they will be able to withhold service charges
- provide that it will be a criminal offence to fail without reasonable excuse to use separate client accounts
- provide that service charges are held in trust, even where only one leaseholder has to pay them
- enable leaseholders to inspect the insurance policy for the insurance for their building, without having first to ask for a summary of the cover. Leaseholders can take copies or have copies provided to them for a reasonable fee
- extend the existing definition of service charges to cover improvements, and allow it to be further extended by regulations
- give leaseholders a new right to challenge unreasonable administration charges payable under the lease
- simplify and strengthen the existing right of leaseholders to be consulted about major works. The requirement to consult leaseholders about major works would apply when the amount payable by any leaseholder exceeds a prescribed sum
- introduce a new requirement for landlords to consult before entering into contracts for the provision of ongoing works or services lasting for longer than 12 months. Disputes over compliance with the requirements would be transferred from the courts to the Leasehold valuation Tribunals.

Leasehold Houses

The Act introduces a number of changes to the rights for leaseholders of houses. The new rights, which amend the 1967 Leasehold reform Act, are as follows:

- The residence test is replaced with a new requirement that the leaseholder must have held the   lease for at least two years.

- The low rent test is abolished.
- Leaseholders can buy the freehold of their property once the lease is extended.
- Where marriage value is payable, it will be split 50%-50% between leaseholder and landlord.
- Marriage value is disregarded where the lease has over 80 years left to run.
- The rights of those who inherit a leasehold house are improved.
- Where leaseholders extend the lease but do not buy the freehold they will become entitled to an assured tenancy under part 1 of the Housing Act 1988 when their extended lease expires.
- The Act includes sub-tenants who would not otherwise qualify.

Absent landlords

The bill also simplifies the procedures for enfranchisement of houses where the landlord cannot be traced. Leaseholders can apply to a county court (rather than the High Court) for a vesting order.

Leasehold Valuation Tribunals will determine the price payable rather than a surveyor appointed by the Lands Tribunal as is the current procedure.

Ground rent and forfeiture

Most long residential leases require an annual ground rent to be paid. The new Act will provide:

- that a leaseholder should only be liable for any ground rent payable under the lease if a written demand has been received from the landlord.
- That the landlord would be prohibited by law from making any additional charge in respect of the rent if the rent is paid within 30 days.

- That the landlord would also be prevented from starting forfeiture action for non-payment of ground rent unless a demand has been made and at least 30 days have elapsed since the demand.

Forfeiture
The new Act will:

- Introduce new restrictions on the commencement of forfeiture proceedings, including the service of notices under section 146 of the Law of Property Act 1925. Landlords can only take action for forfeiture when a court or LVT has determined that a breach of covenant or condition of the lease has occurred. This new provision will address the problem of landlords who threaten forfeiture proceedings on spurious grounds in order to persuade leaseholders to pay unreasonable charges.

Leasehold Valuation Tribunals
Leasehold Valuation Tribunals currently deal with a wide range of disputes involving residential leasehold property. For example they deal with disputes over valuation for purposes of enfranchisement and lease renewal. In addition, they deal with service charge disputes. The new Act introduces changes to the LVT' s designed to make them more effective.

The new Act:

- consolidates the law on the LVT' s procedure and constitution
- extends the LVT's j urisdiction to be able to make a determination as to the liability of leaseholders to pay the service charge.
- Allow landlords to apply to the LVT, before carrying out specific works, for a determination that the costs of the specific works fall to be paid by way of service charges under the relevant leases.

- Allows the LVT to make determinations as to the liability to pay an administration charge.
- Grant the LVT's powers to enforce directions.
- Grant the LVT power to award costs where, in the opinion of the tribunal, a party has in bringing or conducting proceedings before the Tribunal acted frivolously, vexatiously, abusively, disruptively or otherwise unreasonably.
- Provide that all appeals to the Lands Tribunal from the LVT be subject to permission of the LVT concerned or the Lands Tribunal.
- Provide that where both parties agree disputes can be dealt with by way of written representation.

Variation of leases and appointment of a manager

Leaseholders enjoy rights under part 1V of the Landlord and Tenant Act 1987 to seek variations to their leases. The new Act has introduced measures to improve the operation of these rights. In relation to lease variation, the new Act will:

- transfer jurisdiction for applications to vary leases from county courts to Leasehold Valuation Tribunals
- clarify and extend the grounds for applying for a variation of a lease, such as leases that did not provide for a building to be insured under a single policy
- provide a right for any party to a lease of a dwelling to apply to an LVT for an order varying the provisions of a lease on the grounds that a fixed administration charge specified in the lease, or a formula for determining such a charge, was unreasonable

Leaseholders currently enjoy rights to seek the appointment of a new manager under Part 2 of the 1996 Act. The bill contains measures to improve the operation of that right.

Amendments to the appointment for a Manager Regime

Amendments will:

- make clear that leaseholders can apply to a LVT for the appointment of a new manager where a lease provides for management functions to be carried out by a third party manager rather than the landlord
- provide that failure to hold service charge funds in trust or in a separate client account will be a specific ground on which to seek the appointment of a new manager
- restrict the current exemption for resident landlords in converted houses. The exemption would in future not apply if at least half of the flats in the building are held on long leases which are not business tenancies under part 2 of the Landlord and Tenant Act 1954.

The above represents a summary of the changes to the law affecting leaseholders as a result of the introduction of the Commonhold and Leasehold Reform Act 2002.

6

THE FORMATION OF A FLAT MANAGEMENT COMPANY

Flat owners, although individuals in their own right, are joined in the need to ensure that the management of their flats and common areas is carried out cost effectively and efficiently. So far, in this book we have concentrated on the rights and obligations of leaseholders and freeholders. However, if leaseholders wish to exercise the right to enfranchise, as described in the previous chapter, or to simply purchase the freehold on offer from the landlord, then a vehicle for the ownership of the freehold and the management of the flats, will need to be created.

Each flat owner will want to ensure that a proper structure is in place for management and for enforcing obligations between flat owners and for how the building as a whole is maintained and ensured.

What is the purpose of a company set up to manage flats?
At the beginning of the book, the nature of a lease was outlined. Under the terms of flat leases, the flat owner will have entered into covenants which are inserted in the lease and are necessary for the efficient running of the block. Without some separate body enforcing the covenants, management of the building would break down. The block would soon fall into disrepair, the common areas remain unclean and untended and the overall appearance of the block would diminish, along with the value of the properties.

Although there are a number of ways of managing a block of flats, or a house split into flats, such as an individual ownership of the freehold, it is the flat management company which is the recommended vehicle for management of the freehold, after enfranchisement or a straight purchase of the freehold. For the rest of this chapter we will discuss the setting up of such a company and how to go about administering it.

The management company

The company set up to own the freehold and to manage the leases and provide services will be a limited liability company. A limited company is a distinct entity having a separate legal capacity from its shareholders, or members. The company's members have control of the company which they exercise through voting rights. The company may be limited by shares or by guarantee.

A limited company is defined by the concept of limited liability which means that the liability of the members to contribute to the debts of the company is limited. They will have either purchased shares in the company or guaranteed to contribute a fixed sum to the company.

In many cases, a proportion of flat owners in a block will not be interested in participating as members of a company, even though they own a share. Ultimate success of a flat management company will, usually, depend on the will and drive of a few members. Without this drive then the company will not come into being and effective management will not be delivered.

If enough members are enthusiastic then a committee will need to be formed with delegated powers to be able to go forward and set up the limited company. A solicitor will need to be appointed to incorporate the company and to transfer ownership of the freehold from the freeholder to the management company. There will be a number of supporting requirements for the company such as:

- Banking facilities- the committee will need to arrange for a current account to be set up with a local bank, agree signatories to the account and provide the signed mandate for the bank. The bank will offer you further advice;

- Accountants will need to be appointed. This will certainly be the case where there is a lot of money flowing through the company and VAT is involved. If the cash flow is minimal then it may be the case that simple accounts are kept by the members of the committee, by someone with the requisite skills. However, this is a function that will need to be decided as soon as possible.
- The registered office will need to be decided upon.

Other areas of administration may be printed letterheads. Again, some thought should be given as to whether this is really necessary.

A company will have memoranda and articles of association. (see appendix 2). The memoranda and articles of association regulate the activities of the company and define what it can and cannot do. Flat management companies will usually have specific provisions in the articles, limiting membership of the company to those who own a flat in the block or house. Standard forms of articles used by flat management companies can be purchased from any legal stationers, such as OYEZ, based in Holborn, London.

Transferring ownership of the freehold to the new company

The solicitor acting on behalf of the flat owners in the conveyance of the freehold will have a duty to determine good title to the building. All aspects of the ownership of the building and any future matters that may affect ownership will be checked. Many of the tasks undertaken by a solicitor will be the same as if a property was being purchased in the normal way. Local authority searches will be undertaken and questions asked relating to any outstanding debts. The lease will be examined, with a particular emphasis on the provisions for payment of service charges and ground rent, when and how these should be paid and the financial year relating to the company. Of importance here is the question of conveyance of the freehold whilst there are outstanding arrears. Does the newly formed management company wish to undertake responsibility for outstanding arrears or will it insist that these are paid up before transfer? This is an important point and it is good practice to ensure that all arrears are paid up so that the company and its members are starting from a clean slate.

Appointment of officers

It is more than likely that all flat owners will be shareholders of the management company. As with all companies, shareholders will delegate the running of the company to appointed officers. This is necessary as otherwise the whole operation can lose focus and also disagreements can set in.

Companies have a minimum legal requirement on formation-there must be at least two officers at formation, a Director and a Company secretary. There need only be one director in office at any one time. The role of the company secretary is of particular importance as this person has the most work to do in administering the company, giving notice to the members of meetings, preparing notices, drafting resolutions, preparing minutes and filing all statutory forms. The latter task is important because failure to file accounts and annual returns to companies house results in an automatic fine, currently one hundred pounds.

The full details of companies house, the address and supporting information will be given on incorporation of the company.

Most flat management companies, following incorporation, are best managed by a small committee of flat owners, with officers appointed to carry out specific tasks. This committee can rotate on a periodic basis, if needs be.

Common administrative requirements of a flat management company are as follows:

- Insurance
- Maintenance and repairs
- Banking
- Rent and service charge collection

- Preparation of annual budget estimates
- Maintenance of books and accounts
- Annual audit and annual accounts
- Security of property
- Keeping flat owners informed as to the management

It is also very important that all members of the flat management company have read and understand the lease as the lease will define the scope of landlord and leaseholder obligations. For example, repairing obligations are clearly outlined in leases and the policy of the landlord, and the ultimate strategy concerning repairs will need to be defined by the contents of the lease. Some leases will state that a landlord is responsible for all repairs to the structure and exterior of the property, including window frames and front doors. Other leases will limit that responsibility to the structure and exterior, excluding window frames. Ultimately, the policies and practice adopted by the management company will affect how much money is spent and by whom. To repeat, all policy of the management company must be formulated in accordance with the requirements of the lease and this must be clearly communicated to residents.

Insurance considerations

Insurance is normally collected through a service charge. The lease will, in nearly all cases, impose an insurance obligation on the landlord. The insurance will cover the main structure of the building and also public liability. As we have seen, leaseholders have the right to question insurance premiums. However, one advantage of being a shareholder in a company that owns the freehold is that you have complete control of the costs of insurance.

All leaseholders must be aware of the insurance policy, what it covers and how to claim in the event of an insurable loss. Likewise, the officer delegated to look after insurance must be fully acquainted with the nature of the policy and must be prepared to renegotiate the policy every year, ensuring value for money and the best possible cover.

Maintenance and repairs.

The management company, through the freeholders obligations in the lease, will have responsibility for the structure and exterior of the block. As we have seen, this will be more specifically defined in the lease. The management company will be responsible for the foundations of the block, external walls, roof and other supporting structures. In addition, any lifts or other machinery will be the responsibility of the company along with the general maintenance of the common parts. This will include boundary fences and drainage external to flats.

This particular task, and planning for future payments is onerous. The director dealing with maintenance will need to take on board the following points:

- A full assessment of the companies liabilities for repair and maintenance will need to be undertaken through an analysis of the lease. This will need to be summarised and communicated to all leaseholders
- Quotations for work will need to be obtained before works are carried out. The director dealing with this will need to be fully acquainted with the provisions of Landlord and Tenant Acts as outlined earlier in this book. This is of fundamental importance. Remember, any money spent over a certain amount cannot be recovered unless the law has been adhered to. The important exception is emergencies.

The anticipation of future expenditure is very important in respect of future requirements. A decision has to be made as to whether leaseholders are charged as and when works are needed or whether a monthly "sin king fund" is levied, through the service charge, in order to cater for any future expenditure. Remember that any money raised must be placed on an interest bearing account and placed in trust. Your bank can advise you on this aspect. The main point is to have some idea of requirements over the long term, say 25 years and to work out how much money will be needed to cater for this. This method of planning is infinitely more preferable to charging as and when repairs are needed, as money may not be available at this point and management problems may occur. Money paid into a sinking fund is not recoverable by individual leaseholders on sale as this payment is for wear and tear and belongs to the company.

Banking
Money needs to be collected from flat owners, either by standing order or direct debit and receipts issued. The director responsible for banking will usually hold the mandate for cheque signing, along with at least one other person. Authorisation for signing cheques should never be vested in one person as this can lead to misappropriation of funds. The person dealing with banking will probably also be the person dealing with the overall treasury side of the business, including accounts and book keeping.

Rent and Service charge collection
This is usually delegated to one person. Without doubt, the best way to collect service charges and ground rent is through direct debit on a periodic basis, usually monthly. A healthy cash balance is always necessary in order to meet bills.

Preparation of annual budgets
Each year, an assessment of the likely expenditure for the forthcoming financial year will need to be undertaken. This will mean scrutinising the expenditure to date and assessing next years expenditure on the basis of this. Where very heavy costs are anticipated, usually on an item of major repair, all leaseholders will

need to be informed. As described above, if there is money in the pot to deal with it, life becomes that much easier than if all flat owners are to be billed.

One important point: short term thinking, resulting in short term savings for leaseholders is the very worst way of managing the economic process relating to property management. A monthly major repairs charge, through the service charge is, in the view of the author, absolutely necessary.

When it is prepared the budget must be given to all leaseholders (whether members of the company or not) and a clear month should be allowed for any feedback. In reality, with everyone so close to the process, then agreement can be reached before this time. When the budget has been accepted then a copy will need to be sent to all leaseholders, as the final copy and instructions given concerning the changing of direct debits.

If the management company is in the position of having no money to hand to carry out works and the billing of individual leaseholders is necessary then particular care should be taken to ensure that people are in receipt of clear advice concerning the amount for the work, their contribution, when it needs to be paid and how they can raise the money needed. It could be that advice needs to be given about loans, arrangements can be made to spread the payments over several years and so on. It really depends on the situation of the management company concerned. Again, if you can avoid getting into this position through prudent management of charges, then life will be that much easier. A model service charge budget and accounts are shown at the end of the chapter.

Maintenance of accounting records

This function will be performed (preferably) by the same director who deals with other financial matters. In addition, the supervision of the preparation of annual accounts will be undertaken by the same person.

Security of property

This will normally be the responsibility of the person responsible for maintenance and repairs. Security will vary depending on the size and nature of the block of flats in question.

Keeping flat owners informed

Without doubt, one of the major problems in all organisations is that of communication, keeping others informed. If this can be achieved successfully then management becomes that much easier. One person will usually be appointed to do this.

Directors meetings

Directors of flat management companies should aim to have at least two formal meetings a year to review the operations of the company. Of course, meetings will be held informally at different times to discuss various issues. These should always be minuted. However, the six monthly meetings constitute formal meetings of directors. The company secretary will attend such meetings and will minute the proceedings and the minutes of the last meeting will need to be approved and signed as an accurate record. Some decisions may require a vote, which can be the majority of those present, with the chair holding a casting vote in cases of deadlock.

The chairman is usually appointed by the board to oversee the proceedings of the meetings.

Shareholders meetings

Meetings of the shareholders or members are known as general meetings. General meetings of a company is where the formal business of the company is conducted. All members of the company are entitled to attend and they are empowered to vote on certain matters. There are two types of meeting, the annual general meeting and the extraordinary general meeting.

The annual general meeting is where the directors of a company will subject themselves to the scrutiny of its members. It is necessary, by law, for a company to hold an AGM once every calendar year. The first AGM of a newly incorporated company will not be held until 18 months after incorporation.

Each subsequent AGM must happen not more than 15 months after the last one. Details concerning the nature, frequency and type of meeting can be obtained from companies house.

The company secretary will call the AGM, the notice stating the following:

- A statement that the meeting is an AGM
- Details of the meeting, date, time and place
- An agenda of the business to be dealt with
- Details of the rights of members to appoint proxies to vote

This notice is served on all directors, members and auditors of the company. 21 days clear notice must be given of the AGM. If accounts are being presented at the meeting then copies have to be circulated with the notice.

The usual business of an AGM is as follows:

- Election of officers
- Presentation of accounts
- Appointment of auditors
- Directors reports

Any other business should be allowed for at the end. Certain people may have grievances and it is good practice to allow these to be aired.

The articles of association will provide details of a necessary quorum in order to enable the meeting to proceed and decisions to be taken. Minutes must be kept and an annual return, which will normally be sent to the company will need to be submitted to companies house along with the accounts.

The meeting of members other than the AGM is known as an extraordinary general meeting. This is hardly ever necessary. However, the facility for such a meeting does exist. The extraordinary general meeting would only be called in rare circumstances, such as the need to change an aspect of the running of the company which needs urgent agreement, this being the winding up of the company, a serious financial crisis and so on.

The company secretary will send a notice to members and can dispense with the notice period if necessary. The business at the EGM is transacted by the shareholders voting on whichever resolutions are proposed.

See overleaf for a model service charge budget and accounts.

Model service charge budget

ESTIMATE OF SERVICE CHARGES-VICTORIA HOUSE, ALBERT ROAD, WALLINFORD. PERIOD 2001/2002

This estimate of charges has been prepared in accordance with the Landlord And Tenant Acts 1985 and 1987.

Period 5th April 2001 to 31st March 2002.

Charges 2002/2003	Current year charges	Charges
Cleaning of common parts		
Gardening		
Electricity		
Gas		
Insurance		
Day to day maintenance		
Major repairs fund		
Cyclical maintenance (Painting and decorating at three yearly intervals)		
	Total	Total
Number of flats		
Charge per unit	Per annum	
	Per month	

Your landlord is (Registered company)

Notes to above budget. It may be necessary to attach further notes with the budget for information purposes.

Model service charge accounts

(Registered company)

Expenditure statement for 5th April 1999 to 31st March 2000

Victoria House, Albert Road, Wallinford.

Service charge expenditure:

Cleaning of common parts
Gardening
Electricity
Gas
Insurance
Day to day maintenance
Major repairs fund
Cyclical maintenance

Total expenditure

Proportion payable in respect of

Less money paid on account

Balance due

Add ground rent for coming year
Any other

Note that this is a simple form of accounts for example only. It is highly likely that an accountant will prepare a form of accounts for leaseholders.

GLOSSARY OF TERMS

Assignment The transfer of a lease or tenancy from one person to another, usually by sale.

Blanket condition A term in a lease or tenancy that, if taken literally, would impose unreasonable constraints on the use of the premises.

Conveyance The transfer of a freehold from one person to another, usually by sale.

Determination A lease or tenancy is said to be determined when it is brought to an end by a positive act by either the landlord (freeholder) or tenant (leaseholder), as opposed to coming to an end because its term has expired. An outstanding example of a word used in one way by lawyers and another by everyone else.

Enfranchisement (individual) A lease is enfranchised when the leaseholder acquires the freehold. This has the effect of ending the lease and leaving the former leaseholder in sole possession of the freehold.

Enfranchisement (collective) The acquisition of the freehold on behalf of a number of leaseholders acting together.

Exclusive possession The right of a leaseholder or tenant to exclude other people, especially the landlord or freeholder, from the property.

Extension A lease is said to be extended when a longer term is agreed by both parties or (more usually) when it is replaced by a fresh lease with longer to run. The latter can happen either by agreement or as a result of the leaseholder exercising legal rights.

Fixed term A fixed term tenancy or lease is one with a defined ending date, as opposed to a periodic tenancy.

Forfeiture The ultimate penalty if the leaseholder has breached the terms of the lease: the courts can end it and return the property to the freeholder.

Freeholder The owner of the strongest title to land available under English law. Freehold is tantamount to outright ownership and is treated as such in this book. The term 'freeholder' is used throughout to refer to the person granting the lease, although this will not always be the case in practice in practice - see the section on *Head leases and subleases* in Chapter One.

Ground Rent A usually notional payment required under a lease, a source of income to the freeholder and a reminder to the leaseholder that he does not own the property outright.

Head lease When a leaseholder grants one or more subleases, the original lease is called the head lease.

Landlord The granter of a lease, tenancy, or licence.

Lease Strictly, the terms lease and tenancy are interchangeable. In this book, a lease is a tenancy with a fixed term of over seven years.

Leaseholder In this book, a tenant for a fixed term exceeding seven years.

Leasehold valuation tribunal A special committee appointed to settle disputes between freeholders and leaseholders arising from the enfranchisement or extension of leases under the 1967, 1987, and 1993 Acts.

Licence Permission to occupy land not amounting to a tenancy or lease, usually because exclusive possession is not granted.

Long lease Defined for various purposes under the 1967, 1987, and 1993 Acts as a lease originally granted for a fixed term of over 21 years.

Low rent A level of rent defined in the 1967, 1987, and 1993 Acts in ways that are intended to exclude the rent likely to be paid under a periodic tenancy or short fixed term tenancy.

Managing agent An organisation or (seldom) individual appointed by a freeholder to carry out some or all of his management responsibilities.

Management agreement Legal contract appointing a managing agent.

Management fee Payment due from the freeholder to the managing agent.

Marriage value Value by which the elements brought together by a lease enfranchisement, or extension, exceed their combined value as separate entities before it took place. The marriage value is sometimes a component in calculating the premium when leases are extended or enfranchised.

Mixed tenure A mixed tenure block is one that contains both leasehold and tenanted property.

Mortgagee The person or (usually) financial institution lending money against the security of property. Not to be confused with the following.

Mortgagor The owner of property, using it as security to raise a loan. 'Mortgagee' and 'mortgagor' are often confused, but if it is remembered that the owner of the property can be said to have mortgaged it, the difference becomes clear.

Nominee purchaser Whoever is chosen by the leaseholders involved in collective enfranchisement to be the new owner of the freehold: usually a company they have set up for the purpose.

Onerous condition A term in a lease or tenancy that seriously affects its market value.

Open market value The value of any saleable item assuming a willing seller and a willing buyer. The open market value of a freehold or a lease is a component in calculating the premium when leases are extended or enfranchised.

Peppercorn A notional rent is often called a peppercorn - an unusually fanciful piece of legal jargon..

Period of grace Leases sold under the right to buy, and occasionally other leases, contain an estimate of future service charges, usually for the first five years of the lease. During this 'period of grace' any spending above the estimate cannot be recovered.

Periodic A periodic tenancy is one that runs from period to period (usually week to week or month to month) until something intervenes to stop it: the opposite of a fixed term tenancy.

Pre-charging Charging for services in advance: used to build up a sinking fund.

Premium The payment due by the leaseholder to the freeholder when a lease is enfranchised or extended.

Qualifying leaseholders (or qualifying tenants) The tenants or leaseholders that qualify for the various rights, under the 1967, 1987, or 1993 Acts, to enfranchise or extend leases. The qualifications vary depending which right is being exercised under which Act.

Quiet enjoyment The right of leaseholders and tenants not to have their use of the property interfered with by the landlord: closely allied to exclusive possession.

Recognised tenants' association Body of leaseholders and/or tenants recognised by the freeholder for consultation purposes.

Re-entry Regaining possession of a property, for instance at the end of a tenancy or lease.

Rent Payment of (almost always) money in exchange for being allowed to occupy property under a lease, tenancy, or licence.

Residence test Requirement for most purposes under the 1967, 1987, and 1993 Acts that a leaseholder must live on the premises, or have done so in the recent past. The exact test varies depending which right is being exercised.

Reversioner The person to whom possession will revert when the existing lease or tenancy comes to an end; usually the freeholder.

Right to buy A scheme, originally under the Housing Act 1980, allowing tenants of local authorities and some housing associations to buy their homes at a substantial discount.

Service charge Payment by leaseholders and tenants for services provided by the freeholder.

Shared ownership A scheme for assisted house purchase on part-buy, part-rent terms.

Sinking fund A fund built up on the service charge account by pre-charging.

Staircasing The purchase by a shared owner of an additional share of the property.

Sublease A lease granted by a leaseholder.

Tenant For the purpose of this book, someone holding a periodic tenancy or a tenancy granted for a fixed term of less than seven years.

Term The time for which a lease or fixed term tenancy will run.

Appendix 1 Service Charges-The Legal Framework

The Landlord and Tenant Act 1985 section 18-30
The Landlord and Tenant Act 1987 s41-44

Landlord and Tenant Act 1985   c. 70

17.—(1) In proceedings in which a tenant of a dwelling alleges Specific a breach on the part of his landlord of a repairing covenant performance relating to any part of the premises in which the dwelling is of landlord's comprised, the court may order specific performance of the repairing covenant whether or not the breach relates to a part of the premises let to the tenant and notwithstanding any equitable rule restricting the scope of the remedy, whether on the basis of a lack of mutuality or otherwise.

(2) In this section—

(a) " tenant " includes a statutory tenant,

(b) in relation to a statutory tenant the reference to the premises let to him is to the premises of which he is a statutory tenant,

(c) " landlord ", in relation to a tenant, includes any person against whom the tenant has a right to enforce a repairing covenant, and

(d) " repairing covenant " means a covenant to repair, maintain, renew, construct or replace any property.

Service charges

18.—(1) In the following provisions of this Act " service Meaning of charge " means an amount payable by a tenant of a flat as " service part of or in addition to the rent— charge " and " relevant

(a) which is payable, directly or indirectly, for services, costs ". repairs, maintenance or insurance or the landlord's costs of management, and

(b) the whole or part of which varies or may vary according to the relevant costs.

(2) The relevant costs are the costs or estimated costs incurred or to be incurred by or on behalf of the landlord, or a superior landlord, in connection with the matters for which the service charge is payable.

(3) For this purpose—

(a) " costs " includes overheads, and

(b) costs are relevant costs in relation to a service charge whether they are incurred, or to be incurred, in the period for which the service charge is payable or in an earlier or later period.

19.—(1) Relevant costs shall be taken into account in deter- Limitation of mining the amount of a service charge payable for a period— service charges:

(a) only to the extent that they are reasonably incurred, reasonable-and ness.

(b) where they are incurred on the provision of services or the carrying out of works, only if the services or works are of a reasonable standard ;

and the amount payable shall be limited accordingly.

(2) Where a service charge is payable before the relevant costs are incurred, no greater amount than is reasonable is so payable, and after the relevant costs have been incurred any necessary adjustment shall be made by repayment, reduction or subsequent charges or otherwise.

1950 c. 27.

(3) An agreement by the tenant of a flat (other than an arbitration agreement within the meaning of section 32 of the Arbitration Act 1950) is void in so far as it purports to provide for a determination in a particular manner, or on particular evidence, of any question—

    (a) whether costs incurred for services, repairs, maintenance, insurance or management were reasonably incurred,

    (b) whether services or works for which costs were incurred are of a reasonable standard, or

    (c) whether an amount payable before costs are incurred is reasonable.

(4) A county court may make a declaration—

    (a) that any such costs were or were not reasonably incurred,

    (b) that any such services or works are or are not of a reasonable standard, or

    (c) that any such amount is or is not reasonable,

notwithstanding that no other relief is sought in the proceedings.

Limitation of service charges: estimates and consultation.

20.—(1) Where relevant costs incurred on the carrying out of works on a building exceed the limit specified in subsection (2), the excess shall not be taken into account in determining the amount of a service charge unless—

    (a) the requirements of subsection (3) as to estimates and consultation have been complied with, or

    (b) those requirements have been dispensed with by the court in accordance with subsection (5) ;

and the amount payable shall be limited accordingly.

(2) The limit is whichever is the greater of—

    (a) £25, or such other amount as may be prescribed by order of the Secretary of State, multiplied by the number of flats in the building, or

    (b) £500, or such other amount as may be so prescribed.

(3) The requirements are: —

(a) At least two estimates for the works shall be obtained, one of them from a person wholly unconnected with the landlord.

(b) A notice accompanied by a copy of the estimates shall be given to each of the tenants concerned or shall be displayed in the buildings so as to be likely to come to the notice of all those tenants; and, if there is a recognised tenants' association for the building, the notice and copy of the estimates shall also be given to the secretary of the association.

(c) The notice shall describe the works to be carried out and invite observations on them and on the estimates and shall state the name and the address in the United Kingdom of the person to whom the observations may be sent and the date by which they are to be received.

(d) The date stated in the notice shall not be earlier than one month after the date on which the notice is given or displayed as required by paragraph (b).

(e) The landlord shall have regard to any observations received in pursuance of the notice; and unless the works are urgently required they shall not be begun earlier than the date specified in the notice.

(4) For the purposes of subsection (3) the tenants concerned are all the landlord's tenants of flats in the building by whom a service charge is payable to which the costs of the proposed works are relevant.

(5) In proceedings relating to a service charge the court may, if satisfied that the landlord acted reasonably, dispense with all or any of the requirements of subsection (3).

(6) An order under this section—

(a) may make different provision with respect to different cases or descriptions of case, including different provision for different areas, and

(b) shall be made by statutory instrument which shall be subject to annulment in pursuance of a resolution of either House of Parliament.

21.—(1) A tenant may require the landlord in writing to supply him with a written summary of the costs incurred·— *Request for summary of relevant costs.*

(a) if the relevant accounts are made up for periods of twelve months, in the last such period ending not later than the date of the request, or

(b) if the accounts are not so made up, in the period of twelve months ending with the date of the request, and which are relevant costs in relation to the service charges payable or demanded as payable in that or any other period.

(2) If there is a recognised tenants' association for the building and the tenant consents, the request may be made by the secretary of the association instead of by the tenant and may then be for the supply of the summary to the secretary.

(3) A request is duly served on the landlord if it is served on—

    (a) an agent of the landlord named as such in the rent book or similar document, or

    (b) the person who receives the rent on behalf of the landlord;

and a person on whom a request is so served shall forward it as soon as may be to the landlord.

(4) The landlord shall comply with the request within one month of the request or within six months of the end of the period referred to in subsection (1)(a) or (b) whichever is the later.

(5) The summary shall set out the costs in a way showing how they are or will be reflected in demands for services charges.

(6) If there are more than four flats in the building or the costs also relate to another building, the summary shall be certified by a qualified accountant as—

    (a) in his opinion a fair summary complying with the requirement of subsection (5), and

    (b) being sufficiently supported by accounts, receipts and other documents which have been produced to him.

Request to inspect supporting accounts &c. 22.—(1) This section applies where a tenant, or the secretary of a recognised tenants' association, has obtained such a summary as is referred to in section 21(1) (summary of relevant costs), whether in pursuance of that section or otherwise.

(2) The tenant, or the secretary with the consent of the tenant, may within six months of obtaining the summary require the landlord in writing to afford him reasonable facilities—

    (a) for inspecting the accounts, receipts and other documents supporting the summary, and

    (b) for taking copies or extracts from them.

(3) A request under this section is duly served on the landlord if it is served on—

    (a) an agent of the landlord named as such in the rent book or similar document, or

    (b) the person who receives the rent on behalf of the landlord;

Landlord and Tenant Act 1985   c. 70

28.—(1) The reference to a "qualified accountant" in sec- Meaning of
tion 21(6) (certification of summary of information about rele- "qualified
vant costs) is to a person who, in accordance with the following accountant".
provisions, has the necessary qualification and is not disqualified
from acting.

(2) A person has the necessary qualification if he is a member
of one of the following bodies—

    the Institute of Chartered Accountants in England and
      Wales.
    the Institute of Chartered Accountants in Scotland,
    the Association of Certified Accountants,
    the Institute of Chartered Accountants in Ireland, or
    any other body of accountants established in the United
      Kingdom and recognised by the Secretary of State for
      the purposes of section 389(1)(a) of the Companies Act 1985 c. 6.
      1985,

or if he is a person who is for the time being authorised by the
Secretary of State under section 389(1)(b) of that Act (or the
corresponding provision of the Companies Act 1948) as being 1948 c. 38.
a person with similar qualifications obtained outside the United
Kingdom.

(3) A Scottish firm has the necessary qualification if each
of the partners in it has the necessary qualification.

(4) The following are disqualified from acting—

    (a) a body corporate, except a Scottish firm ;
    (b) an officer or employee of the landlord or, where the
      landlord is a company, of an associated company ;
    (c) a person who is a partner or employee of any such
      officer or employee.

(5) For the purposes of subsection (4)(b) a company is associated with a landlord company if it is (within the meaning of
section 736 of the Companies Act 1985) the landlord's holding
company, a subsidiary of the landlord or another subsidiary
of the landlord's holding company.

(6) Where the landlord is a local authority, a new town cor-
poration or the Development Board for Rural Wales—

    (a) the persons who have the necessary qualification in-
      clude members of the Chartered Institute of Public
      Finance and Accountancy, and
    (b) subsection (4)(b) (disqualification of officers and em-
      ployees of landlord) does not apply.

Meaning of
" recognised
tenants'
association ".

29.—(1) A recognised tenants' association is an association of tenants of flats in a building which is recognised for the purposes of the provisions of this Act relating to service charges either—

    (a) by notice in writing given by the landlord to the secretary of the association, or

    (b) by a certificate of a member of the local rent assessment committee panel.

(2) A notice given under subsection (1)(a) may be withdrawn by the landlord by notice in writing given to the secretary of the association not less than six months before the date on which it is to be withdrawn.

(3) A certificate given under subsection (1)(b) may be cancelled by any member of the local rent assessment committee panel.

(4) In this section the " local rent assessment committee panel " means the persons appointed by the Lord Chancellor under the Rent Act 1977 to the panel of persons to act as members of a rent assessment committee for the registration area in which the building is situated.

(5) The Secretary of State may by regulations specify the matters to which regard is to be had in giving or cancelling a certificate under subsection (1)(b).

(6) Regulations under subsection (5)—

    (a) may make different provisions with respect to different cases or descriptions of case, including different provision for different areas, and

    (b) shall be made by statutory instrument which shall be subject to annulment in pursuance of a resolution of either House of Parliament.

Meaning of
" flat ",
" landlord "
and " tenant ".

30. In the provisions of this Act relating to service charges—

  " flat " means a separate set of premises, whether or not on the same floor, which—

    (a) forms part of a building,

    (b) is divided horizontally from some other part of the building, and

    (c) is constructed or adapted for use for the purposes of a dwelling and is occupied wholly or mainly as a private dwelling;

  " landlord " includes any person who has a right to enforce payment of a service charge;

  " tenant " includes

    (a) a statutory tenant, and

    (b) where the flat or part of it is sub-let, the sub-tenant.

and, in a case where a variation is so modified, subsections (1) and (2) above shall, as from the date when the modification takes effect, apply to the variation as modified. PART IV

Applications relating to dwellings other than flats

40.—(1) Any party to a long lease of a dwelling may make an application to the court for an order varying the lease, in such manner as is specified in the application, on the grounds that the lease fails to make satisfactory provision with respect to any matter relating to the insurance of the dwelling, including the recovery of the costs of such insurance. *Application for variation of insurance provisions of lease of dwelling other than a flat.*

(2) Sections 36 and 38 shall apply to an application under subsection (1) subject to the modifications specified in subsection (3).

(3) Those modifications are as follows—

   (a) in section 36—

      (i) in subsection (1), the reference to section 35 shall be read as a reference to subsection (1) above, and

      (ii) in subsection (2), any reference to a flat shall be read as a reference to a dwelling; and

   (b) in section 38—

      (i) any reference to an application under section 35 shall be read as a reference to an application under subsection (1) above, and

      (ii) any reference to an application under section 36 shall be read as a reference to an application under section 36 as applied by subsection (2) above.

(4) For the purposes of this section a long lease shall not be regarded as a long lease of a dwelling if the demised premises consist of or include the dwelling and one or more other dwellings; and this section does not apply to a long lease of a dwelling if it constitutes a tenancy to which Part II of the Landlord and Tenant Act 1954 applies (other than an assured tenancy as defined in section 56(1) of the Housing Act 1980). 1954 c. 56.
1980 c. 51.

(5) In this section "dwelling" means a dwelling other than a flat.

PART V

MANAGEMENT OF LEASEHOLD PROPERTY

Service charges

41.—(1) Sections 18 to 30 of the 1985 Act (regulation of service charges payable by tenants) shall have effect subject to the amendments specified in Schedule 2 (which include amendments— *Amendments relating to service charges.*

   (a) extending the provisions of those sections to dwellings other than flats, and

   (b) introducing certain additional limitations on service charges).

98

(2) Sections 45 to 51 of the Housing Act 1985 (which are, so far as relating to dwellings let on long leases, superseded by sections 18 to 30 of the 1985 Act as amended by Schedule 2) shall cease to have effect in relation to dwellings so let.

Service charge contributions to be held in trust.

42.—(1) This section applies where the tenants of two or more dwellings may be required under the terms of their leases to contribute to the same costs by the payment of service charges; and in this section—

"the contributing tenants" means those tenants;

"the payee " means the landlord or other person to whom any such charges are payable by those tenants under the terms of their leases;

"relevant service charges" means any such charges;

1977 c. 42.

"service charge" has the meaning given by section 18(1) of the 1985 Act, except that it does not include a service charge payable by the tenant of a dwelling the rent of which is registered under Part IV of the Rent Act 1977, unless the amount registered is, in pursuance of section 71(4) of that Act, entered as a variable amount;

"tenant" does not include a tenant of an exempt landlord; and

"trust fund" means the fund, or (as the case may be) any of the funds, mentioned in subsection (2) below.

(2) Any sums paid to the payee by the contributing tenants by way of relevant service charges, and any investments representing those sums, shall (together with any income accruing thereon) be held by the payee either as a single fund or, if he thinks fit, in two or more separate funds.

(3) The payee shall hold any trust fund—

(a) on trust to defray costs incurred in connection with the matters for which the relevant service charges were payable (whether incurred by himself or by any other person), and

(b) subject to that, on trust for the persons who are the contributing tenants for the time being.

(4) Subject to subsections (6) to (8), the contributing tenants shall be treated as entitled by virtue of subsection (3)(b) to such shares in the residue of any such fund as are proportionate to their respective liabilities to pay relevant service charges.

(5) If the Secretary of State by order so provides, any sums standing to the credit of any trust fund may, instead of being invested in any other manner authorised by law, be invested in such manner as may be specified in the order; and any such order may contain such incidental, supplemental or transitional provisions as the Secretary of State considers appropriate in connection with the order.

(6) On the termination of the lease of a contributing tenant the tenant shall not be entitled to any part of any trust fund, and (except where subsection (7) applies) any part of any such fund which is attributable to relevant service charges paid under the lease shall accordingly continue to be held on the trusts referred to in subsection (3).

(7) If after the termination of any such lease there are no longer any contributing tenants, any trust fund shall be dissolved as at the date of the termination of the lease, and any assets comprised in the fund immediately before its dissolution shall—

    (a) if the payee is the landlord, be retained by him for his own use and benefit, and

    (b) in any other case, be transferred to the landlord by the payee.

(8) Subsections (4), (6) and (7) shall have effect in relation to a contributing tenant subject to any express terms of his lease which relate to the distribution, either before or (as the case may be) at the termination of the lease, of amounts attributable to relevant service charges paid under its terms (whether the lease was granted before or after the commencement of this section).

(9) Subject to subsection (8), the provisions of this section shall prevail over the terms of any express or implied trust created by a lease so far as inconsistent with those provisions, other than an express trust so created before the commencement of this section.

Insurance

43.—(1) The following section shall be inserted after section 30 of the 1985 Act—

"Insurance

30A. The Schedule to this Act- (which confers on tenants certain rights with respect to the insurance of their dwellings) shall have effect."

(2) Schedule 3 to this Act shall be added to the 1985 Act as the Schedule to that Act.

Managing agents

44. The following section shall be inserted in the 1985 Act after the section 30A inserted by section 43—

"Managing agents

30B.—(1) A recognised tenants' association may at any time serve a notice on the landlord requesting him to consult the association in accordance with this section on matters relating to the appointment or employment by him of a managing agent for any relevant premises.

(2) Where, at the time when any such notice is served by a recognised tenants' association, the landlord does not employ any managing agent for any relevant premises, the landlord shall, before appointing such a managing agent, serve on the association a notice specifying—

    (a) the name of the proposed managing agent;

    (b) the landlord's obligations to the tenants represented by the association which it is proposed that the managing agent should be required to discharge on his behalf; and

(c) a period of not less than one month beginning with the date of service of the notice within which the association may make observations on the proposed appointment.

(3) Where, at the time when a notice is served under subsection (1) by a recognised tenants' association, the landlord employs a managing agent for any relevant premises, the landlord shall, within the period of one month beginning with the date of service of that notice, serve on the association a notice specifying—

(a) the landlord's obligations to the tenants represented by the association which the managing agent is required to discharge on his behalf; and

(b) a reasonable period within which the association may make observations on the manner in which the managing agent has been discharging those obligations, and on the desirability of his continuing to discharge them.

(4) Subject to subsection (5), a landlord who has been served with a notice by an association under subsection (1) shall, so long as he employs a managing agent for any relevant premises—

(a) serve on that association at least once in every five years a notice specifying—

(i) any change occurring since the date of the last notice served by him on the association under this section in the obligations which the managing agent has been required to discharge on his behalf; and

(ii) a reasonable period within which the association may make observations on the manner in which the managing agent has discharged those obligations since that date, and on the desirability of his continuing to discharge them;

(b) serve on that association, whenever he proposes to appoint any new managing agent for any relevant premises, a notice specifying the matters mentioned in paragraphs (a) to (c) of subsection (2).

(5) A landlord shall not, by virtue of a notice served by an association under subsection (1), be required to serve on the association a notice under subsection (4)(a) or (b) if the association subsequently serves on the landlord a notice withdrawing its request under subsection (1) to be consulted by him.

(6) Where—

(a) a recognised tenants' association has served a notice under subsection (1) with respect to any relevant premises, and

(b) the interest of the landlord in those premises becomes vested in a new landlord,

that notice shall cease to have effect with respect to those premises (without prejudice to the service by the association on the new landlord of a fresh notice under that subsection with respect to those premises).

(7) Any notice served by a landlord under this section shall specify the name and the address in the United Kingdom of the person to whom any observations made in pursuance of the notice are to be sent; and the landlord shall have regard to any such observations that are received by that person within the period specified in the notice.

(8) In this section—

"landlord", in relation to a recognised tenants' association, means the immediate landlord of the tenants represented by the association or a person who has a right to enforce payment of service charges payable by any of those tenants;

"managing agent", in relation to any relevant premises, means an agent of the landlord appointed to discharge any of the landlord's obligations to the tenants represented by the recognised tenants' association in question which relate to the management by him of those premises; and

"tenant" includes a statutory tenant;

and for the purposes of this section any premises (whether a building or not) are relevant premises in relation to a recognised tenants' association if any of the tenants represented by the association may be required under the terms of their leases to contribute by the payment of service charges to costs relating to those premises."

Management by registered housing associations

45.—(1) Section 4 of the Housing Associations Act 1985 (eligibility for registration) shall be amended as follows.

(2) In subsection (3) (permissible additional purposes or objects), after the paragraph (dd) inserted by section 19 of the Housing and Planning Act 1986 there shall be inserted—

"(ddd) managing houses which are held on leases (not being houses falling within subsection (2)(a) or (b)) or blocks of flats;".

(3) After that subsection there shall be inserted—

Extension of permissible objects of registered housing associations as regards the management of leasehold property.
1985 c. 69.
1986 c. 63.

Appendix 2

Memorandum and Articles of Association

Company limited by Guarantee
Company Limited by Shares

SHARE COMPANY

THE COMPANIES ACTS 1985 to 1989

PRIVATE COMPANY LIMITED BY SHARES

MEMORANDUM OF ASSOCIATION OF

1. The Company's name is ''.
2. The Company's registered office is to be situated in England and Wales.
3. The Company's objects are:
   (a) (i) To manage and administer the freehold or leasehold property or properties known as

(hereinafter called 'the Estate') and any other land, buildings and real property, either on its own account or as trustee, nominee or agent of any other company or person.

   (ii) To acquire and deal with and take options over any property, real or personal, including the Estate, and any rights or privileges of any kind over or in respect of any property, and to improve, develop, sell, lease, accept, surrender or dispose of or otherwise deal with all or any part of such property and any and all rights of the Company therein or thereto.

   (iii) To collect all rents, charges and other income and to pay any rates, taxes, charges, duties, levies, assessments or other outgoings of whatsoever nature charged, assessed, or imposed on or in respect of the Estate or any part thereof.

   (iv) To provide services of every description in relation to the Estate and to maintain, repair, renew, redecorate, repaint, clean, construct, alter and add to the Estate and to arrange for the supply to it of services and amenities and the maintenance of the same and the cultivation, maintenance, landscaping and planting of any land, gardens and grounds comprised in the Estate and to enter into contracts with builders, tenants, contractors and others and to employ appropriate staff and managing or other agents whatsoever in relation thereto.

   (v) To insure the Estate or any other property of the Company or in which it has an interest against damage or destruction and such other risks as may be considered necessary, appropriate or desirable and to insure the Company against public liability and any other risks which it may consider prudent or desirable to insure against.

(vi) To establish and maintain capital reserves. management funds and any form of sinking fund in order to pay or contribute towards all fees, costs, and other expenses incurred in the implementation of the Company's objects and to require the Members of the Company to contribute towards such reserves or funds at such times. in such amounts and in such manner as the Company may think fit and to invest and deal in and with such moneys not immediately required in such manner as may from time to time be determined.

(b) To carry on any other trade or business whatever which can in the opinion of the Board of Directors be advantageously carried on in connection with or ancillary to any of the businesses of the Company.

(c) To improve, manage, construct, repair, develop, exchange, let on lease or otherwise, mortgage, charge, sell, dispose of, turn to account, grant licences, options, rights and privileges in respect of, or otherwise deal with all or any part of the property and rights of the Company.

(d) To invest and deal with the moneys of the Company not immediately required in such manner as may from time to time be determined and to hold or otherwise deal with any investments made.

(e) To lend and advance money or give credit on any terms and with or without security to any person, firm or company, to enter into guarantees, contracts of indemnity and suretyships of all kinds, to receive money on deposit or loan upon any terms, and to secure or guarantee in any manner and upon any terms the payment of any sum of money or the performance of any obligation by any person, firm or company.

(f) To borrow and raise money in any manner and to secure the repayment of any money borrowed, raised or owing by mortgage, charge, standard security, lien or other security upon the whole or any part of the Company's property or assets (whether present or future), including its uncalled capital, and also by a similar mortgage, charge, standard security, lien or security to secure and guarantee the performance by the Company of any obligation or liability it may undertake or which may become binding on it.

(g) To draw, make, accept, endorse, discount, negotiate, execute and issue cheques, bills of exchange. promissory notes, bills of lading, warrants, debentures, and other negotiable or transferable instruments.

(h) To enter into any arrangements with any government or authority (supreme. municipal, local, or otherwise) that may seem conducive to the attainment of the Company's objects or any of them, and to obtain from any such government or authority any charters, decrees, rights, privileges or concessions which the Company may think desirable and to carry out, exercise. and comply with any such charters, decrees. rights, privileges, and concessions.

(i) To pay all or any expenses incurred in connection with the promotion, formation and incorporation of the Company, or to contract with any person, firm or company to pay the same. and to pay commissions to brokers and others for underwriting, placing. selling, or guaranteeing the subscription of any shares or other securities of the Company.

(j) To give or award pensions, annuities, gratuities, and superannuation or other allowances or benefits or charitable aid and generally to provide advantages, facilities and services for any persons who are or have been Directors of, or who are or have been employed by, or who are serving or have served the Company and to the wives, widows, children and other relatives and dependants of such persons; to make payments towards insurance: and to set up, establish, support and maintain superannuation and other funds or schemes (whether contributory or non-contributory) for the benefit of any of such persons and of their wives, widows, children and other relatives and dependants.

(k) Subject to and in accordance with a due compliance with the provisions of Sections 155 to 158 (inclusive) of the Act (if and so far as such provisions shall be applicable), to give, whether directly or indirectly, any kind of financial assistance (as defined in Section 152(1)(a) of the Act) for any such purpose as is specified in Section 151(1) and/or Section 151(2) of the Act.

(l) To distribute among the Members of the Company in kind any property of the Company of whatever nature.

(m) To do all or any of the things or matters aforesaid in any part of the world and either as principals, agents, contractors or otherwise, and by or through agents, brokers, sub-contractors or otherwise and either alone or in conjunction with others.

(n) To do all such other things as may be deemed incidental or conducive to the attainment of the Company's objects or any of them.

AND so that:

(1) None of the objects set forth in any sub-clause of this Clause shall be restrictively construed but the widest interpretation shall be given to each such object, and none of such objects shall, except where the context expressly so requires. be in any way limited or restricted by reference to or inference from any other object or objects set forth in such sub-clause, or by reference to or inference from the terms of any other sub-clause of this Clause, or by reference to or inference from the name of the Company.

(2) None of the sub-clauses of this Clause and none of the objects therein specified shall be deemed subsidiary or ancillary to any of the objects specified in any other such sub-clause, and the Company shall have as full a power to exercise each and every one of the objects specified in each sub-clause of this Clause as though each such sub-clause contained the objects of a separate Company.

(3) The word 'Company' in this Clause, except where used in reference to the Company, shall be deemed to include any partnership or other body of persons, whether incorporated or unincorporated and whether domiciled in the United Kingdom or elsewhere.

(4) In this Clause the expression 'the Act' means the Companies Act 1985, but so that any reference in this Clause to any provision of the Act shall be deemed to include a reference to any statutory modification or re-enactment of that provision for the time being in force.

4. The liability of the Members is limited.

5. The Company's share capital is   divided into   shares of   each.

THE COMPANIES ACTS 1985 to 1989

PRIVATE COMPANY LIMITED BY SHARES

ARTICLES OF ASSOCIATION OF

PRELIMINARY

1. (a) The Regulations contained in Table A in the Schedule to the Companies (Tables A to F) Regulations 1985 (SI 1985 No. 805) as amended by the Companies (Tables A to F) (Amendment) Regulations 1985 (SI 1985 No. 1052) (such Table being hereinafter called 'Table A') shall apply to the Company save in so far as they are excluded or varied hereby and such Regulations (save as so excluded or varied) and the Articles hereinafter contained shall be the regulations of the Company.

(b) In these Articles:

'the Act'   means the Companies Act 1985, but so that any reference in these Articles to any provision of the Act shall be deemed to include a reference to any statutory modification or re-enactment of that provision for the time being in force.

'the Estate'   shall have the meaning assigned to it in the Memorandum of Association but shall also include any other land. building or premises for the time being also owned and/ or managed or administered by the Company;

'dwelling'   means any residential unit comprised in the Estate:

'dwellingholder'   means the person or persons to whom a lease or tenancy of a dwelling has been granted or assigned or who holds the freehold of a dwelling and so that whenever two or more persons are for the time being dwellingholders of a dwelling they shall for all purposes of these Articles be deemed to constitute one dwellingholder.

ALLOTMENT AND TRANSFER OF SHARES

2. (a) The subscribers to the Memorandum of Association of the Company shall be duly registered as Members of the Company in respect of the

shares for which they have subscribed. A subscriber may transfer any shares subscribed by him to a person nominated by him in writing to succeed him as a Member and any such person (other than a dwellingholder) so nominated shall have the same power to transfer the share as if he had himself been a subscriber. Personal representatives of a deceased subscriber or of any successor so nominated by him shall have the same rights of transfer.

(b) Save as aforesaid, no share shall be allotted or transferred to any person who is not a dwellingholder. A dwellingholder shall not be entitled to dispose of his shareholding in the Company while holding, whether alone or jointly with others, a legal estate in any dwelling.

(c) In accordance with Section 91(1) of the Act Sections 89(1) and 90(1) to (6) (inclusive) of the Act shall not apply to the Company.

(d) Subject as provided in paragraph (b) above the Directors are generally and unconditionally authorised for the purposes of Section 80 of the Act, to exercise any power of the Company to allot and grant rights to subscribe for or convert securities into shares of the Company up to the amount of the authorised share capital with which the Company is incorporated at any time or times during the period of five years from the date of incorporation and the Directors may, after that period, allot any shares or grant any such rights under this authority in pursuance of an offer or aggreement so to do made by the Company within that period. The authority hereby given may at any time (subject to the said Section 80)'be renewed, revoked or varied by Ordinary Resolution of the Company in General Meeting.

3. (a) If any Member of the Company who is a dwellingholder parts with all interest in the dwelling or dwellings held by him, or if his interest therein for any reason ceases and determines, he or, in the event of his death, his legal personal representative or representatives, or in the event of his bankruptcy, his trustee in bankruptcy shall transfer his shareholding in the Company to the person or persons who become the dwellingholder of his dwelling or dwellings. .

(b) Each subscriber to the Memorandum of Association and any person becoming a Member as a result of a nomination under Article 2(a) shall, if not himself a dwellingholder, offer his shareholding in the Company to the Company as soon as dwellingholders for all the dwellings have become Members. The Company shall:

(i) subject to the provisions of the Act, purchase such shareholding in which case the Member concerned shall execute all such documents (including any contract required under Section 164 of the Act) and do all such acts and things as may be necessary in order to enable the Company to comply with the Act and effect such purchase: or

(ii) direct the Member concerned to transfer his shareholding to some other dwellingholder or dwellingholders in which case the Member concerned shall execute a share transfer in respect of his shareholding as appropriate and deliver the same to the Company PROVIDED that the sanction of a Special Resolution shall be required for any such transfer where the proposed transferee or transferees already hold one share of the Company in respect of each of their dwellings.

(c) The price to be paid on the transfer of every share under this Article shall, unless (in the case of a transfer made pursuant to paragraph (a) above) the transferor and transferee otherwise agree, be its nominal value.

(d) If the holder of a share (or his legal personal representative or representatives or trustee in bankruptcy) refuses or neglects to transfer it or offer it for purchase in accordance with this Article, one of the Directors, duly nominated for that purpose by a Resolution of the Board, shall be the attorney of such holder, with full power on his behalf and in his name to execute, complete and deliver a transfer of his share to the person or persons to whom the same ought to be transferred hereunder or (as the case may be) any documentation as is referred to in paragraph (b) above; and the Company may give a good discharge for the purchase money and (in the case of a transfer) enter the name of the transferee of the said share in the Register of Members as the holder thereof.

4. If a Member shall die or be adjudged bankrupt, his legal personal representative or representatives or the trustee in his bankruptcy shall be entitled to be registered as a Member of the Company, provided he or they shall for the time being be a dwellingholder.

5. (a) The Directors shall refuse to register any transfer of shares made in contravention of all the foregoing provisions of these Articles, but otherwise shall have no power to refuse to register a transfer.

(b) Clause 24 in Table A shall not apply to the Company.

SHARES

6. The lien conferred by Clause 8 in Table A shall attach also to fully paid-up shares, and the Company shall also have a first and paramount lien on all shares, whether fully paid or not, standing registered in the name of any person indebted or under liability to the Company, whether he shall be the sole registered holder thereof or shall be one of two or more joint holders, for all moneys presently payable by him or his estate to the Company. Clause 8 in Table A shall be modified accordingly.

7. The liability of any member in default in respect of a call shall be increased by the addition at the end of the first sentence of Clause 18 in Table A of the words 'and all expenses that may have been incurred by the Company by reason of such non-payment'.

GENERAL MEETINGS AND RESOLUTIONS

8 Every notice convening a General Meeting shall comply with the provisions of Section 372(3) of the Act as to giving information to Members in

regard to their right to appoint proxies; and notices of and other communications relating to any General Meeting which any Member is entitled to receive shall be sent to the Directors and to the Auditors for the time being of the Company.

9. (a) If a quorum is not present within half an hour from the time appointed for a General Meeting the General Meeting shall stand adjourned to the same day in the next week at the same time and place or to such other day and at such other time and place as the Directors may determine; and if at the adjourned General Meeting a quorum is not present within half an hour from the time appointed therefor such adjourned General Meeting shall be dissolved.

(b) Clause 41 in Table A shall not apply to the Company.

VOTES OF MEMBERS

10. (a) Every Member present in person or by proxy at a General Meeting shall have one vote PROVIDED that where no dwellingholder exists in respect of any dwelling, those Members who are subscribers to the Memorandum of Association or who became Members as a result of having been nominated under Article 2(a) or, if there is only one such Member or person nominated under Article 2(a), that Member, shall, either jointly if there is more than one such Member, or alone, if there is only one such Member, have three votes in respect of every dwelling in addition to their own vote or votes as Members.

(b) Clause 54 in Table A shall not apply to the Company.

APPOINTMENT OF DIRECTORS

11. (a) Clause 64 in Table A shall not apply to the Company.

(b) The maximum number and minimum number respectively of the Directors may be determined from time to time by Ordinary Resolution in General Meeting of the Company. Subject to and in default of any such determination there shall be no maximum number of Directors and the minimum number of Directors shall be two.

(c) The Directors shall not be required to retire by rotation and Clauses 73 to 80 (inclusive) in Table A shall not apply to the Company.

(d) Save for the persons who are deemed to have been appointed as the first Directors of the Company on incorporation pursuant to Section 13(5) of the Act, no person who is not a Member of the Company shall in any circumstances be eligible to hold office as a Director. Clause 44 in Table A shall not apply to the Company.

(e) No Member shall be appointed a Director at any General Meeting unless either:

(i) he is recommended by the Directors; or

(ii) not less than fourteen nor more than thirty-five clear days before

111

the date appointed for the General Meeting, notice signed by a Member qualified to vote at the General Meeting has been given to the Company of the intention to propose that Member for appointment, together with notice signed by that Member of his willingness to be appointed.

(f) Subject to paragraph (e) above, the Company may by Ordinary Resolution in General Meeting appoint any Member who is willing to act to be a Director, either to fill a vacancy or as an additional Director.

(g) The Directors may appoint a Member who is willing to act to be a Director, either to fill a vacancy or as an additional Director, provided that the appointment does not cause the number of Directors to exceed any number determined in accordance with paragraph (b) above as the maximum number of Directors and for the time being in force.

BORROWING POWERS

12. The Directors may exercise all the powers of the Company to borrow money without limit as to amount and upon such terms and in such manner as they think fit, and subject (in the case of any security convertible into shares) to Section 80 of the Act to grant any mortgage, charge or standard security over its undertaking, property and uncalled capital, or any part thereof, and to issue debentures, debenture stock, and other securities whether outright or as security for any debt, liability or obligation of the Company or of any third party.

ALTERNATE DIRECTORS

13. (a) No person who is not a Member of the Company shall be capable of being appointed an alternate Director. Clause 65 in Table A shall be modified accordingly.

(b) An alternate Director shall not be entitled as such to receive any remuneration from the Company, save that he may be paid by the Company such part (if any) of the remuneration otherwise payable to his appointor as such appointor may by notice in writing to the Company from time to time direct, and the first sentence of Clause 66 in Table A shall be modified accordingly.

(c) A Director, or any other Member approved by resolution of the Directors and willing to act, may act as an alternate Director to represent more than one Director, and an alternate Director shall be entitled at any meeting of the Directors or of any committee of the Directors to one vote for every Director whom he represents in addition to his own vote (if any) as a Director, but he shall count as only one for the purpose of determining whether a quorum is present.

DISQUALIFICATION OF DIRECTORS

14. The office of a Director shall be vacated if he ceases to be a member of the Company and Clause 81 in Table A shall be modified accordingly.

GRATUITIES AND PENSIONS

15. (a) The Directors may exercise the powers of the Company conferred by Clause 3(j) of the Memorandum of Association of the Company and shall be entitled to retain any benefits received by them or any of them by reason of the exercise of any such powers.
    (b) Clause 87 in Table A shall not apply to the Company.

PROCEEDINGS OF DIRECTORS

16. (a) A Director may vote, at any meeting of the Directors or of any committee of the Directors, on any resolution, notwithstanding that it in any way concerns or relates to a matter in which he has, directly or indirectly, any kind of interest whatsoever, and if he shall vote on any such resolution as aforesaid his vote shall be counted; and in relation to any such resolution as aforesaid he shall (whether or not he shall vote on the same) be taken into account in calculating the quorum present at the meeting.
    (b) Clauses 94 to 97 (inclusive) in Table A shall not apply to the Company.

THE SEAL

17. If the Company has a seal it shall only be used with the authority of the Directors or of a committee of Directors. The Directors may determine who shall sign any instrument to which the seal is affixed and unless otherwise so determined it shall be signed by a Director and by the Secretary or second Director. The obligation under Clause 6 of Table A relating to the sealing of share certificates shall apply only if the Company has a seal. Clause 101 of Table A shall not apply to the Company.

INDEMNITY

18. (a) Every Director or other officer or Auditor of the Company shall be indemnified out of the assets of the Company against all losses or liabilities which he may sustain or incur in or about the execution of the duties of his office or otherwise in relation thereto, including any liability incurred by him in defending any proceedings, whether civil or criminal, in which judgment is given in his favour or in which he is acquitted or in connection with any application under Section 144 or Section 727 of the Act in which relief is granted to him by the Court, and no Director or other officer shall be liable

for any loss, damage or misfortune which may happen to or be incurred by the Company in the execution of the duties of his office or in relation thereto. But this Article shall only have effect in so far as its provisions are not avoided by Section 310 of the Act.

(b) The Directors shall have power to purchase and maintain for any Director, officer or Auditor of the Company insurance against any such liability as is referred to in Section 310(1) of the Act from and after the bringing into force of Section 137 of the Companies Act 1989.

(c) Clause 118 in Table A shall not apply to the Company.

RULES OR BYELAWS

19. The Directors may from time to time make such Rules or Byelaws as they may deem necessary or expedient or convenient for the proper conduct and management of the Company and for the purposes of prescribing the classes of and conditions of membership, and in particular but without prejudice to the generality of the foregoing, they shall by such Rules or Byelaws regulate:-

(i) the admission and classification of Members of the Company, and the rights and privileges of such Members, and the conditions of membership and the terms on which Members may resign or have their membership terminated and the entrance fees, subscriptions and other fees, charges, contributions or payments to be made by Members;

(ii) the conduct of Members of the Company in relation to one another, and to the Company and to the Company's servants or agents;

(iii) the setting aside of the whole or any part or parts of the Estate at any particular time or times or for a particular purpose or purposes;

(iv) the procedure at General Meetings and Meetings of the Directors and committees of the Directors of the Company insofar as such procedure is not regulated by these Articles:

(v) and, generally, all such matters as are commonly the subject matter of Company Rules or rules or regulations appropriate to property of a similar nature and type as the Estate.

The Company in General Meeting shall have power to alter or repeat the Rules or Byelaws and to make additions thereto and the Directors shall adopt such means as they deem sufficient to bring to the notice of Members of the Company all such Rules or Byelaws, which so long as they shall be in force, shall be binding on all Members of the Company. Provided, nevertheless, that no Rule or Byelaw shall be inconsistent with, or shall affect or repeal anything contained in, the Memorandum or Articles of Association of the Company.

GUARANTEE COMPANY

THE COMPANIES ACTS 1985 to 1989

COMPANY LIMITED BY GUARANTEE
AND NOT HAVING A SHARE CAPITAL

MEMORANDUM OF ASSOCIATION OF

·1. The Company's name is "

2. The Company's registered office is to be situated in England and Wales.

3. The Company's objects are:-

(a) (i) To manage and administer the freehold or leasehold property or properties known as

(hereinafter called 'the Estate') and any other land, buildings and real property, either on its own account or as trustee, nominee or agent of any other company or person.

(ii) To acquire and deal with and take options over any property, real or personal, including the Estate, and any rights or privileges of any kind over or in respect of any property, and to improve, develop, sell, lease, accept. surrender or dispose of or otherwise deal with all or any part of such property and any and all rights of the Company therein or thereto.

(iii) To collect all rents, charges and other income and to pay any rates, taxes, charges. duties, levies, assessments or other outgoings of whatsoever nature charged, assessed. or imposed on or in respect of the Estate or any part thereof.

(iv) To provide services of every description in relation to the Estate and to maintain, repair, renew, redecorate. repaint, clean, construct, alter and add to the Estate and to arrange for the supply to it of services and amenities and the maintenance of the same and the cultivation, mainte-nance. landscaping and planting of any land. gardens and grounds comprised in the Estate and to enter into contracts with builders, tenants, contractors and others and to employ appropriate staff and managing or other agents whatsoever in relation thereto.

(v) To insure the Estate or any other property of the Company or in which it has an interest against damage or destruction and such other risks as may be considered necessary, appropriate or desirable and to insure the Company against public liability and any other risks which it may consider prudent or desirable to insure against.

(vi) To establish and maintain capital reserves, management funds and any form of sinking fund in order to pay or contribute towards all fees, costs, and other expenses incurred in the implementation of the Company's objects and to require the Members of the Company to contribute towards such reserves or funds at such times, in such amounts and in such manner as the Company may think fit and to invest and deal in and with such moneys not immediately required in such manner as may from time to time be determined.

(b) To carry on any other trade or business whatever which can in the opinion of the Board of Directors be advantageously carried on in connection with or ancillary to any of the businesses of the Company.

(c) To improve, manage, construct, repair, develop, exchange, let on lease or otherwise, mortgage, charge, sell, dispose of, turn to account, grant licences, options, rights and privileges in respect of, or otherwise deal with all or any part of the property and rights of the Company.

(d) To invest and deal with the moneys of the Company not immediately required in such manner as may from time to time be determined and to hold or otherwise deal with any investments made.

(e) To lend and advance money or give credit on any terms and with or without security to any person, firm or company, to enter into guarantees, contracts of indemnity and suretyships of all kinds, to receive money on deposit or loan upon any terms, and to secure or guarantee in any manner and upon any terms the payment of any sum of money or the performance of any obligation by any person, firm or company.

(f) To borrow and raise money in any manner and to secure the repayment of any money borrowed, raised or owing by mortgage, charge, standard security, lien or other security upon the whole or any part of the Company's property or assets (whether present or future), and also by a similar mortgage, charge, standard security, lien or security to secure and guarantee the performance by the Company of any obligation or liability it may undertake or which may become binding on it.

(g) To draw, make, accept, endorse, discount, negotiate, execute and issue cheques, bills of exchange, promissory notes, bills of lading, warrants, debentures, and other negotiable or transferable instruments.

(h) To enter into any arrangements with any government or authority (supreme, municipal, local, or otherwise) that may seem conducive to the attainment of the Company's objects or any of them, and to obtain from any such government or authority any charters, decrees, rights, privileges or concessions which the Company may think desirable and to carry out, exercise, and comply with any such charters, decrees, rights, privileges, and concessions.

(i) To pay all or any expenses incurred in connection with the promotion,

:ormation and incorporation of the Company, or to contract with any person, firm or company to pay the same.

(j) To give or award pensions, annuities, gratuities, and superannuation or other allowances or benefits or charitable aid and generally to provide advantages, facilities and services for any persons who are or have been Directors of, or who are or have been employed by, or who are serving or have served the Company and to the wives, widows, children and other relatives and dependants of such persons; to make payments towards insurance; and to set up, establish, support and maintain superannuation and other funds or schemes (whether contributory or non-contributory) for the benefit of any of such persons and of their wives, widows, children and other relatives and dependants.

(k) To distribute among the Members of the Company in kind any property of the Company of whatever nature.

(l) To do all or any of the things or matters aforesaid in any part of the world and either as principals, agents, contractors or otherwise, and by or through agents, brokers, sub-contractors or otherwise and either alone or in conjunction with others.

(m) To do all such other things as may be deemed incidental or conducive to the attainment of the Company's objects or any of them.

AND so that:-

(1) None of the objects set forth in any sub-clause of this Clause shall be restrictively construed but the widest interpretation shall be given to each such object, and none of such objects shall, except where the context expressly so requires, be in any way limited or restricted by reference to or inference from any other object or objects set forth in such sub-clause, or by reference to or inference from the terms of any other sub-clause of this Clause, or by reference to or inference from the name of the Company.

(2) None of the sub-clauses of this Clause and none of the objects therein specified shall be deemed subsidiary or ancillary to any of the objects specified in any other such sub-clause, and the Company shall have as full a power to exercise each and every one of the objects specified in each sub-clause of this Clause as though each such sub-clause contained the objects of a separate Company.

(3) The word 'Company' in this Clause, except where used in reference to the Company, shall be deemed to include any partnership or other body of persons, whether incorporated or unincorporated and whether domiciled in the United Kingdom or elsewhere.

(4) In this Clause the expression 'the Act' means the Companies Act 1985, but so that any reference in this Clause to any provision of the Act shall be deemed to include a reference to any statutory modification or re-enactment of that provision for the time being in force.

4. The liability of the Members is limited.

5. Every Member of the Company undertakes to contribute such amount as may be required (not exceeding £1) to the Company's assets if it should

be wound up while he is a member or within one year after he ceases to be a Member, for payment of the Company's debts and liabilities contracted before he ceases to be a Member, and of the costs, charges and expenses of winding up, and for the adjustment of the rights of the contributories among themselves.

THE COMPANIES ACTS 1985 to 1989

COMPANY LIMITED BY GUARANTEE
AND NOT HAVING A SHARE CAPITAL

ARTICLES OF ASSOCIATION OF

PRELIMINARY

1. (a) The Regulations contained in Table A in the Schedule to the Companies (Table A to F) Regulations 1985 (SI 1985 No. 805) as amended by the Companies (Tables A to F) (Amendment) Regulations 1985 (SI 1985 No. 1052) (such Table being hereinafter called 'Table A') shall apply to the Company save in so far as they are excluded or varied hereby and such Regulations (save as so excluded or varied) and the Articles hereinafter contained shall be the regulations of the Company.

(b) Clauses 2 to 35 (inclusive), 57, 59, 102 to 108 (inclusive), 110, 114, 116 and 117 in Table A shall not apply to the Company.

INTERPRETATION

2. (a) In these Articles:

'the Act' means the Companies Act 1985, but so that any reference in these Articles to any provision of the Act shall be deemed to include a reference to any statutory modification or re-enactment of that provision for the time being in force.

'the Estate' shall have the meaning assigned to it in the Memorandum of Association but shall also include any other land, building or premises for the time being also owned and/ or managed or administered by the Company;

'dwelling' means any residential unit comprised in the Estate;

'dwellingholder' means the person or persons to whom a lease or tenancy of a dwelling has been granted or assigned or who holds the freehold of a dwelling and so that whenever two or more persons are for the time being dwellingholders of a dwelling they shall for all purposes of these Articles be deemed to constitute one dwellingholder.

(b) Clause 1 in Table A shall be read and construed as if the definition of 'the holder' were omitted therefrom.

MEMBERS

3. The subscribers to the Memorandum of Association shall be Members of the Company. A subscriber may nominate any person to succeed him as a Member of the Company and any person so nominated (other than a dwellingholder) shall have the same power to nominate a person to succeed him as if he had been a subscriber. Save as aforesaid, no person shall be admitted as a Member of the Company other than a dwellingholder. The Company must accept as a Member every person who is or who shall have become entitled to be admitted as a Member and shall have complied with either of the signature provisions set out in Article 5.

4. Each subscriber to the Memorandum of Association and any person nominated to be a Member under Article 3 shall, if not himself a dwellingholder, cease to be a Member as soon as dwellingholders for all the dwellings have become Members.

5. The provisions of Section 352 of the Act shall be observed by the Company and every Member of the Company other than the subscribers to the Memorandum of Association shall either sign a written consent to become a Member or sign the Register of Members on becoming a Member. If two or more persons are together a dwellingholder each shall so comply, they shall together constitute one Member and the person whose name first appears in the Register of Members shall exercise the voting powers vested in such Member.

6. A dwellingholder shall cease to be a Member on the registration as a Member of the successor to his dwelling and shall not resign as a Member while holding, whether alone or jointly with others, a legal estate in any dwelling.

7. If a Member shall die or be adjudged bankrupt his legal personal representative or representatives or the trustee in his bankruptcy shall be entitled to be registered as a Member provided that he or they shall for the time being be a dwellingholder.

GENERAL MEETINGS AND RESOLUTIONS

8. (a) An Annual General Meeting and an Extraordinary General Meeting called for the passing of a Special Resolution or a Resolution appointing a member as a Director shall be called by at least 21 clear days' notice. All other Extraordinary General Meetings shall be called by at least 14 clear days' notice but a General Meeting may be called by shorter notice if it is so agreed:

(i) in the case of an Annual General Meeting, by all the Members entitled to attend and vote thereat; and

(ii) in the case of any other General Meeting, by a majority in number of the Members having a right to attend and vote, being a majority together holding (subject to the provisions of any elective resolution of the Company for the time being in force) not less than ninety-five per cent of the total voting rights at the Meeting of all the Members.

(b) The notice shall specify the time and place of the Meeting and, in the case of an Annual General Meeting, shall specify the Meeting as such.

(c) The notice shall be given to all the Members and to the auditors and to every person, being a legal personal representative or a trustee in bankruptcy of a Member where the Member, but for his death or bankruptcy, would be. entitled to receive notice of the Meeting.

(d) Clause 38 in Table A shall not apply to the Company.

(e) Any Member of the Company entitled to attend and vote at a General Meeting shall be entitled to appoint another person (whether a Member or not) as his proxy to attend and vote instead of him and any proxy so appointed shall have the same right as the Member to speak at the Meeting. Every notice convening a General Meeting shall comply with the provisions of Section 372(3) of the Act as to giving information to Members in regard to their right to appoint proxies.

9. (a) If a quorum is not present within half an hour from the time appointed for a General Meeting the General Meeting shall stand adjourned to the same day in the next week at the same time and place or to such other day and at such other time and place as the Directors may determine; and if at the adjourned General Meeting a quorum is not present within half an hour from the time appointed therefor such adjourned General Meeting shall be dissolved.

(b) Clause 41 in Table A shall not apply to the Company.

10. Clause 46 in Table A shall be read and construed as if paragraph (d) was omitted therefrom.

VOTES OF MEMBERS

11. (a) Every Member present in person or by proxy at a General Meeting shall have one vote PROVIDED that where no dwellingholder exists in respect of any dwelling, those Members who are subscribers to the Memorandum of Association or who became Members as a result of having been nominated by a subscriber to the Memorandum of Association under Article 3 or, if there is only one such Member or person nominated under Article 3, that Member, shall, either jointly if there is more than one such Member, or alone, if there is only one such Member, have three votes in respect of every dwelling in addition to their own vote or votes as Members.

(b) Clauses 54 and 55 in Table A shall not apply to the Company.

APPOINTMENT OF DIRECTORS

12. (a) Clause 64 in Table A shall not apply to the Company.

(b) The maximum number and minimum number respectively of the Directors may be determined from time to time by Ordinary Resolution in General Meeting of the Company. Subject to and in default of any such determination there shall be no maximum number of Directors and the minimum number of Directors shall be two.

(c) The Directors shall not be required to retire by rotation and Clauses 73 to 80 (inclusive) in Table A shall not apply to the Company.

(d) Save for the persons who are deemed to have been appointed as the first Directors of the Company on incorporation pursuant to Section 13(5) of the Act, no person who is not a Member of the Company shall in any circumstances be eligible to hold office as a Director. Clause 44 in Table A shall not apply to the Company.

(e) Clause 83 in Table A shall be read and construed as if the words 'of any class of shares or' were omitted therefrom.

(f) No Member shall be appointed a Director at any General Meeting unless either:

(i) he is recommended by the Directors; or

(ii) not less than fourteen nor more than thirty-five clear days before the date appointed for the General Meeting, notice signed by a Member qualified to vote at the General Meeting has been given to the Company of the intention to propose that Member for appointment, together with notice signed by that Member of his willingness to be appointed.

(g) Subject to paragraph (f) above, the Company may by Ordinary Resolution in General Meeting appoint any Member who is willing to act to be a Director, either to fill a vacancy or as an additional Director.

(h) The Directors may appoint a Member who is willing to act to be a Director, either to fill a vacancy or as an additional Director, provided that the appointment does not cause the number of Directors to exceed any number determined in accordance with paragraph (b) above as the maximum number of Directors and for the time being in force.

BORROWING POWERS

13. The Directors may exercise all the powers of the Company to borrow money without limit as to amount and upon such terms and in such manner as they think fit, and to grant any mortgage, charge or standard security over its undertaking and property or any part thereof, and to issue debentures, whether outright or as security for any debt, liability or obligation of the Company or of any third party.

ALTERNATE DIRECTORS

14. (a) No person who is not a Member of the Company shall be capable of being appointed an alternate Director. Clause 65 in Table A shall be modified accordingly.

(b) An alternate Director shall not be entitled as such to receive any remuneration from the Company, save that he may be paid by the Company such part (if any) of the remuneration otherwise payable to his appointor as such appointor may by notice in writing to the Company from time to time direct, and the first sentence of Clause 66 in Table A shall be modified accordingly.

(c) A Director, or any other Member approved by resolution of the Directors and willing to act, may act as an alternate Director to represent more than one Director, and an alternate Director shall be entitled at any meeting of the Directors or of any committee of the Directors to one vote for every Director whom he represents in addition to his own vote (if any) as a Director, but he shall count as only one for the purpose of determining whether a quorum is present.

DISQUALIFICATION OF DIRECTORS

15. The office of a Director shall be vacated if he ceases to be a member of the Company and Clause 81 in Table A shall be modified accordingly.

GRATUITIES AND PENSIONS

16. (a) The Directors may exercise the powers of the Company conferred by Clause 3(j) of the Memorandum of Association of the Company and shall be entitled to retain any benefits received by them or any of them by reason of the exercise of any such powers.

(b) Clause 87 in Table A shall not apply to the Company.

PROCEEDINGS OF DIRECTORS

17. (a) A Director may vote, at any meeting of the Directors or of any committee of the Directors, on any resolution, notwithstanding that it in any way concerns or relates to a matter in which he has, directly or indirectly, any kind of interest whatsoever, and if he shall vote on any such resolution as aforesaid his vote shall be counted; and in relation to any such resolution as aforesaid he shall (whether or not he shall vote on the same) be taken into account in calculating the quorum present at the meeting.

(b) Clauses 94 to 97 (inclusive) in Table A shall not apply to the Company.

MINUTES

18. Clause 100 in Table A shall be read and construed as if the words 'of the holders of any class of shares in the Company' were omitted therefrom.

THE SEAL

19. If the Company has a seal it shall only be used with the authority of the Directors or of a committee of Directors. The Directors may determine who shall sign any instrument to which the seal is affixed and unless otherwise so determined it shall be signed by a Director and by the Secretary or second Director. Clause 101 of Table A shall not apply to the Company.

NOTICES

20. Clause 112 in Table A shall be read and construed as if the second sentence was omitted therefrom.
21. Clause 113 in Table A shall be read and construed as if the words 'or of the holders of any class of shares in the Company' were omitted therefrom.

INDEMNITY

22. (a) Every Director or other officer or Auditor of the Company shall be indemnified out of the assets of the Company against all losses or liabilities which he may sustain or incur in or about the execution of the duties of his office or otherwise in relation thereto, including any liability incurred by him in defending any proceedings, whether civil or criminal, in which judgment is given in his favour or in which he is acquitted or in connection with any application under Section 727 of the Act in which relief is granted to him by the Court, and no Director or other officer shall be liable for any loss, damage or misfortune which may happen to or be incurred by the Company in the execution of the duties of his office or in relation thereto. But this Article shall only have effect in so far as its provisions are not avoided by Section 310 of the Act.

(b) The Directors shall have power to purchase and maintain for any Director, officer or Auditor of the Company insurance against any such liability as is referred to in Section 310(1) of the Act from and after the bringing into force of Section 137 of the Companies Act 1989.

(c) Clause 118 in Table A shall not apply to the Company.

RULES OR BYELAWS

23. The Directors may from time to time make such Rules or Byelaws as they may deem necessary or expedient or convenient for the proper conduct and management of the Company and for the purposes of

prescribing the classes of and conditions of membership, and in particular but without prejudice to the generality of the foregoing, they shall by such Rules or Byelaws regulate:

(i) the admission and classification of Members of the Company, and the rights and privileges of such Members, and the conditions of membership and the terms on which Members may resign or have their membership terminated and the entrance fees, subscriptions and other fees, charges, contributions or payments to be made by Members;

(ii) the conduct of Members of the Company in relation to one another, and to the Company and to the Company's servants or agents;

(iii) the setting aside of the whole or any part or parts of the Estate at any particular time or times or for a particular purpose or purposes;

(iv) the procedure at General Meetings and Meetings of the Directors and committees of the Directors of the Company in so far as such procedure is not regulated by these Articles;

(v) and, generally, all such matters as are commonly the subject matter of Company Rules or rules or regulations appropriate to property of a similar nature and type as the Estate.

The Company in General Meeting shall have power to alter or repeal the Rules or Byelaws and to make additions thereto and the Directors shall adopt such means as they deem sufficient to bring to the notice of Members of the Company all such Rules or Byelaws, which so long as they shall be in force, shall be binding on all Members of the Company. Provided, nevertheless, that no Rule or Byelaw shall be inconsistent with, or shall affect or repeal anything contained in, the Memorandum or Articles of Association of the Company.